Blueprint Remodel

Blueprint Remodel

Tract Home Transformations That Turn Everyday to Extraordinary

Michelle Kodis

Gibbs Smith, Publisher
Salt Lake City

*For Rich—you wrote the book
on following dreams.*

First Edition

08 07 06 05 04   5 4 3 2 1

Text © 2004 Michelle Kodis

Photographs © 2004 as noted throughout

Published by

Gibbs Smith, Publisher

P.O. Box 667

Layton, Utah 84041

Orders: 1.800.748.5439

www.gibbs-smith.com

Cover photo: Weldon Brewster

Back cover photo: Claudio Santini

Detail photo on page 3: Edward Caldwell

Designed and produced by Kurt Wahlner

Printed and bound in Hong Kong

Library of Congress Cataloging-in-Publication Data

Kodis, Michelle.

 Blueprint remodel : tract home transformations that turn everyday to
extraordinary / Michelle Kodis.—1st ed.

    p. cm.

 ISBN 1-58685-372-4

 1. Suburban homes—Remodeling—United States. I. Title.

NA7571.K59 2004

728'.37'0286—dc22   2004005056

Acknowledgments

My thanks and appreciation to

Gibbs Smith, Suzanne Taylor, and Kurt Wahlner—a publishing dream team.

Alison Einerson and her top-notch publicity staff—all books need enthusiastic cheerleaders.

The architects and homeowners who saw the potential in these tract homes and decided to make them magnificent.

The photographers whose images capture the essence of a house reborn.

Robert, Joan, and Steven Kodis and the Cieciuchs, my dear family; Rosemerry, Kendall, Marcia, Donna, Ramona, Susanna, Jean, Duffy, and Susan (aka Super Mom of Aiden and Izzy), a circle of true support; stepsons Andrew and Brett Cieciuch, fast becoming fine young men; Violet and Roscoe.

Contents

Introduction

San Mateo, California
Novato, California
Los Altos, California

Northridge, California

A QUICK WORD of caution: what you are about to see may shock you. Not to worry, though—the shock factor in this book is meant to inspire, not scare. The star of this show is the ordinary American tract house. Criticized and often mercilessly ridiculed, the tract home has a long way to go to improve its placement on the architectural totem pole.

I think it's time for us to change our thinking about this much-maligned dwelling, and to that end I have gathered ten dramatic (and, indeed, sometimes shocking) examples of the untapped potential hidden behind plain white walls, lackluster materials, boxy rooms, and choppy floor plans. The proof is in these pages: even the most lifeless tract house can be magnificently transformed.

Although we tend to look down our noses at tract houses, it's important to recognize they are the result of an inherently good deed: the creation of homes that, while not memorable, made it possible for people from all walks of life to own a home. In their relatively brief history, tract houses have run the gamut from Joseph Eichler's high-style modernist California beauties (now very

9

popular and commanding high prices) to the stamped-out "McMansions" that are rising up in suburbs across the country. Somewhere in between these two extremes is the everyday tract house: the ranch, rambler, split-level, bungalow, ranchette—call it what you like. Regardless of the label, these homes' detailing, materials, and floor plans are likely no different than those of thousands of others. This cookie-cutter method is the essence of the tract house—by keeping them similar or, even, identical, developers can significantly reduce design and construction costs.

The economics driving traditional tract home production (there is an up-and-coming industry that offers customized tract houses) often translate into a spare materiality with few or no embellish-

ments. The floor plans are also designed for speedy completion and typically feature "clusters" of low-ceilinged rooms accessed by dark, narrow hallways. Because careful siting takes time and, thus, money, these homes usually are not positioned to maximize views (if they exist) nor are they mindful of using natural light to brighten and warm the interiors. On the contrary, these homes are placed according to the exact parameters of the tract development layout. What this means is that although at times they occupy beautiful parcels of land, their design prevents their inhabitants from fully enjoying the scenery.

The main problem, though, is obvious: the tract home is just plain boring. Many people desire more than what the tract can offer in its original state. Here is the good news: often, remodeling a tract house makes more financial sense than buying or building a new home. And, it's not uncommon for people to say they like the location of their house—it's the building itself that needs work.

The ten examples that follow reveal what can happen when the blinders are removed and the tract home is viewed in a fresh light. It takes a great deal of vision—and faith—to see beyond the constraints of the tract house, and the architects who conceived and guided these projects are visionaries in their own right. These houses were carefully chosen so you would be able to see and study transformations that have a wide range of cost and scope. You may not want—or need—to overhaul your entire house, and this kind of scaled-down approach is presented here. If you have a tight budget, you will also discover clever low-cost techniques that will be kind to your wallet. Finally, if you are ready to embark on a significant renovation, you will find those ideas here as well. From a one-floor interior makeover in an Omaha tract for a couple of empty-nesters, to a full renovation of a Texas bungalow to accommodate a growing family and home-based business, these examples encompass a variety of challenges and solutions, and they include everything from sleek modern design to a remodel influenced by the Arts and Crafts movement.

My goal with this book is simple: to inspire you to make your tract home your castle.

MICHELLE KODIS

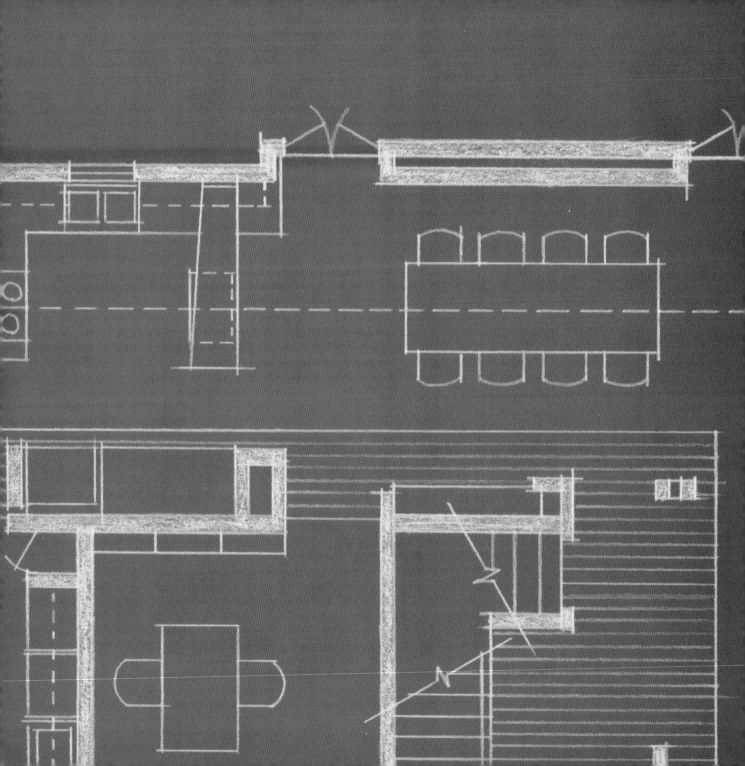

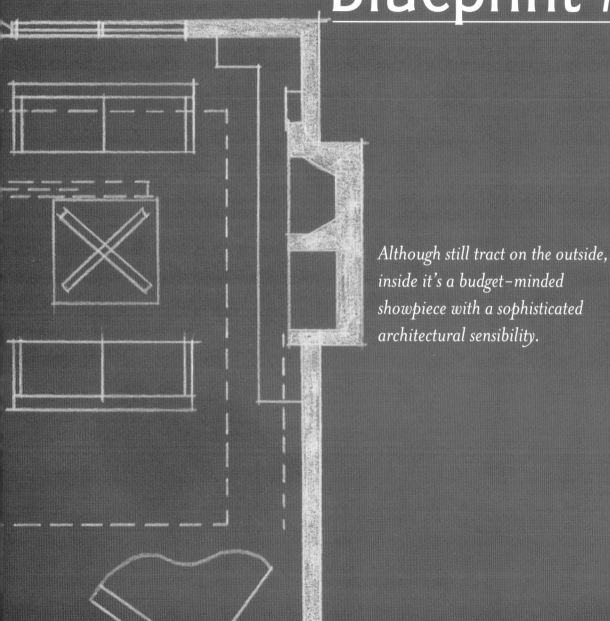

Blueprint # 1

Although still tract on the outside, inside it's a budget-minded showpiece with a sophisticated architectural sensibility.

You Can't Judge This Book by Its Cover

Cost of Remodel: $150,000 in 2002

Architect: Randy Brown, Randy Brown Architects

Exterior and "Before" Photographs: Randy Brown

Interior "After" Photographs: Farshid Assassi

Architect's Transformation Techniques:

—Use a limited palette of affordable materials and repeat them in a variety of ways for consistency in design and color.

—Remove as many walls as possible to open up the floor plan to accommodate the owners' lifestyle.

—Limit the remodel to the first floor to save money and focus on the owners' current needs.

OUTSIDE, IT'S A PLAIN-Jane tract house in an Omaha suburb—the kind that wouldn't merit a second look. Inside, however, the 1960s house is another story altogether: walk through the front door and you are transported into an oasis of contemporary finishes and furnishings and a reconfigured main-level interior that says anything but tract.

Designed by Randy Brown of Omaha-based Randy Brown Architects, the year-long makeover was the request of a couple with grown children. Having lived in the 2,000-square-foot house for more than twenty years, the empty-nesters were ready to embark on a significant change. "All those little rooms no longer worked for their lifestyle, which now

The architect took a flaw and turned it into a design element by wrapping a dropped ceiling around an existing structural wood beam, which during construction was found to have a gap right in the middle. For textural contrast, a section of the beam was left exposed while the rest was covered in drywall and linked to its other half via drywall columns that serve as return air vents for the home's HVAC system. Maple hardwood laminate flooring, factory-finished for cost-effectiveness, identifies circulation patterns (light wood) and areas of function (dark wood).

15

involves a lot of entertaining," Brown says. "But, they were fond of the house and the neighborhood and didn't want to leave." The alternative to relocation was an innovative interpretation of the existing structure that turned it into something special; gone are the claustrophobic rooms, replaced with a streamlined space that easily accommodates social gatherings. Despite a pricey appearance, the entire project, from design to construction and through to furnishings, cost a very reasonable $150,000. Leaving the exterior and second floor as is kept costs

Removing a wall between the dining room and kitchen freed the cramped rooms, and visually "stretching" the space achieved the illusion of greater depth and increased square footage, even though the home's footprint did not change. Visible on the far living room wall, the maple panel that hides the television acts as a focal point to draw the eye through the space. The canopy light fixture above the table is a low-cost ($100) combination of plumbing pipe, maple plywood "ribs" and basic hardware.

From the street, the 1960s house has a typical tract profile.

Omaha Remodel

First Floor After Remodel

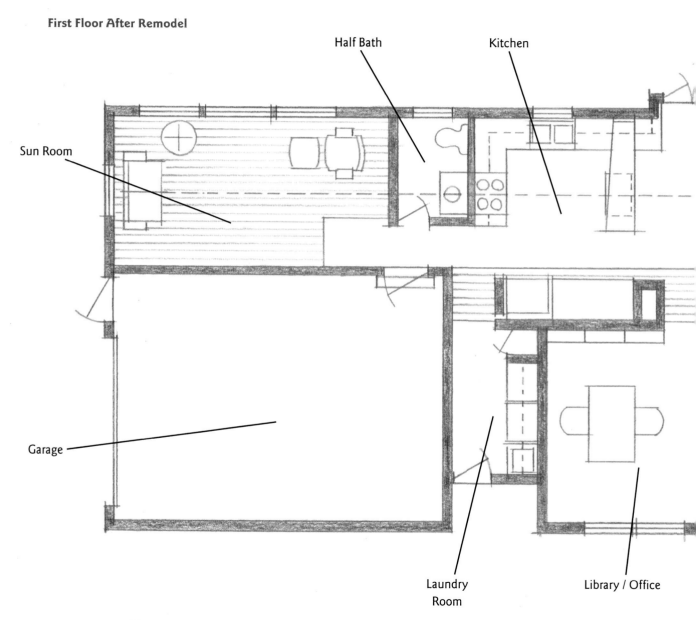

Half Bath

Kitchen

Sun Room

Garage

Laundry Room

Library / Office

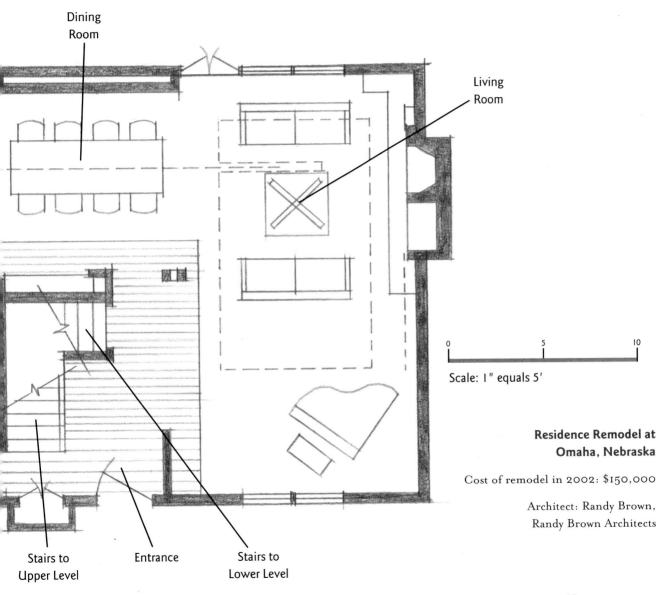

Dining
Room

Living
Room

Stairs to
Upper Level

Entrance

Stairs to
Lower Level

0   5   10

Scale: 1″ equals 5′

**Residence Remodel at
Omaha, Nebraska**

Cost of remodel in 2002: $150,000

Architect: Randy Brown,
Randy Brown Architects

in check, as did the architect's use of economical materials.

From a compositional perspective, the biggest task was figuring out how to rework and redefine the cramped floor plan—typical of many tract homes. This required the removal of most of the interior walls to reveal an open L-shaped plan for the living room, dining room, kitchen, sunroom, and guest bathroom. One of Brown's main challenges surfaced when he took out the wall between the family and living rooms and discovered a large wood timber beam with a gap in it—a flaw in the construction. The beam couldn't be removed because it supported a floor joist, so Brown

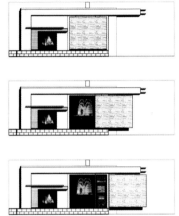

Item of Interest:
The living room sofas are by:
Cassina
www.cassinausa.com

The fireplace, still in its original location, has been given a dramatic makeover with a drywall surround to match the walls, a black slate hearth, a maple mantel, and an L-shaped stainless steel surround detail. The maple panel to the right of the fireplace slides across the television, which now sits in a niche that pops out of the exterior wall. Acrylic panels, fashioned into an L-shaped feature above the fireplace, are backlit with fluorescent bulbs to add soft light to this corner of the room.

Simple, inexpensive materials were brought together in the living room: plumbing pipe (as a ceiling detail and coffee-table base), black slate (hearth), stainless steel (fireplace surround detail), and maple (mantel). Classic white furnishings and walls will remain in style for years to come.

devised a clever way to incorporate it into the remodel: he dropped a ceiling plane beneath it to disguise it, leaving one section exposed for a glimpse of texture in the refined interiors.

When it came time to choose materials, Brown selected a few key thematic elements and repeated them in different ways in different rooms. For example, plumbing pipe found unexpected life in several custom light fixtures and as a ceiling detail and towel rack. Stainless steel serves as the base for the coffee and dining tables and was used for kitchen backsplashes and to make a fireplace surround detail. Black slate is found in the bathroom and at the fireplace hearth, acrylic cabinet fronts were used both in the kitchen and in a built-in shelf in the dining room, and glass is prominent in the bathroom and dining and living rooms.

Heeding the budget, the architect made sure his custom designs were cost-conscious. The canopy light fixtures in the dining room and sunroom were fashioned from lengths of plumbing pipe, maple plywood ribs, and inexpensive hardware for just $100 each. The coffee table is simply a sheet of glass supported by a stainless steel base. "We used some very inexpensive materials in interesting ways," Brown points out. "And, while each room in the original house was separate, now the rooms are trying to be the same via consistency in materials and color. We wanted to achieve a look that wouldn't date itself, and the result is a clean, modern design that is timeless."

Item of Interest:
The "Happy Hour" sunroom loveseat is by:
B&B Italia
www.bebitalia.it

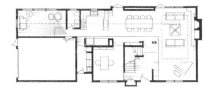

The small double-hung window on the far wall was the only one in what is now the sunroom. The addition of three large maple windows transformed the room into a cozy place to relax and enjoy the warmth of the southwest exposure. Light maple floors and a canopy light fixture complete the look.

A built-in shelf made from three-quarter-inch clear glass suspended from the ceiling with steel cable provides elegant storage, and acrylic-fronted cabinets below appear to float above the floor. The custom dining table was constructed with a stainless steel base and a three-quarter-inch glass top. The room adjoins the new library, previously a formal dining room.

Like the rest of the house, the kitchen incorporates understated materials and design features, including braided steel cable cabinet pulls, a stainless steel backsplash, Corian counters, backlit acrylic-fronted cabinets, and maple French doors, which replaced a set of flimsy sliding doors. The breakfast counter hovers lightly above the dishwasher, now contained within a stainless steel enclosure. To save money, appliances stayed in their original locations and new cabinets and counters were built around them.

Because drop ceiling cabinets made the small kitchen seem even smaller, the architect's challenge was to open up the room without sacrificing storage.

A glass sink and vanity and a
black slate floor repeat the
home's materials theme. The
mirror sits slightly off the wall
and is held up with steel cable.

The kitchen is functional and bright
thanks to practical materials and
crisp lines and forms. During construction, it became apparent that
the kitchen window above the sink
was off-center. To fix it, the architect
placed a solid maple frame against
the window and then cut an opening
for the glass. The result: the window
is now perfectly positioned.

Items of Interest:
The barstools and dining
chairs are by:
AZ Cast
www.azcast.com

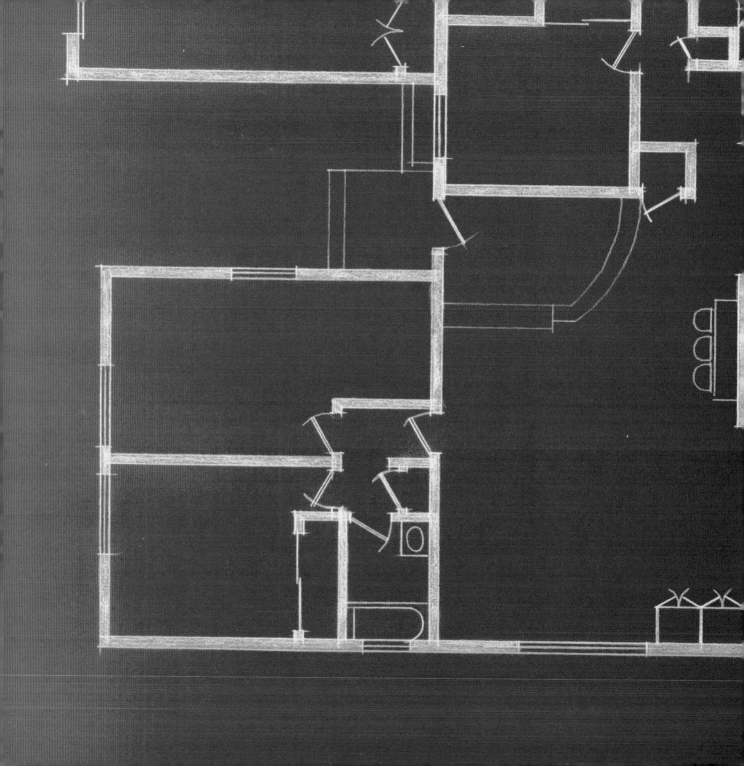

Blueprint #2

Simple materials and clever ideas share the spotlight in this modern reinterpretation of a cookie-cutter tract house.

Adventurous Homeowners Find Their California Dream

Northridge, California

Cost of Remodel: $250,000 in 2002

Architect: John Sofio, Built, Inc.

"Before" Photographs: Courtesy of the owner

"After" Photographs: David Adamson and Harriet Robinson

Architect's Transformation Techniques:

—Create a stronger connection between the indoor and outdoor living spaces with a revamped patio and poolside dining area.

—Remove the low ceiling to bring height to the interior of the one-level house and, outside, add a raised entry platform for visual variation.

—Use inexpensive but beautiful materials in combinations that speak to a minimalist but comfortable aesthetic.

THE OWNERS OF THIS LOW-SLUNG 1970S California tract house were ready for a change but didn't want to spend a fortune and were reluctant to take architectural risks. A number of other homes in their subdivision had been remodeled, and they believed theirs should conform to an unspoken design ethic—which by some accounts wasn't that exciting. Enter John Sofio of the Los Angeles–based Built, Inc. Sofio is known as much for his imaginative approach to design as for his ability to work wonders with a tight budget and a challenging property. Although the owners resisted his preliminary suggestions, he persisted, and soon enough they began to see his logic and agreed to even the boldest moves. "It was my job to convince them to do it differently," he says. "Conformity is indeed a part of this neighborhood, but since there were no actual design guidelines in place, it

The narrow band of slate on the patio is identical to the material used for the interior floors, fostering the illusion of a continuous indoor/outdoor space that is further accentuated by two sets of Douglas fir French doors that swing out to the patio. The cement-block barbecue station has a weather-resistant slate counter and is protected by a roof overhang canted to correspond to the angles of the dormer windows.

was simply conformity by choice. When the owners started to trust my decisions and get excited about them, we were able to break open the floodgates and work together. Today they're in love with the house and are glad they took a few risks." Sofio's course of action was to take the dwelling from plain to exceptional, trimming costs wherever possible by working with the structure and defining and refining the spaces along the way. "This was what I call a broad-stroke remodel," he adds. "We knew we were dealing with a tract house, and the problem was its cookie-cutter personality."

A flat-roofed addition to one end of the previously L-shaped house expanded the

Although the floor plan is now open, the architect incorporated "buffers" to give rooms of differing function a suggestion of separation. The living room and kitchen are set apart subtly by a structural sheer wall (to the left), beneath which is a custom rolling cabinet made from Finlandian birch plywood with a Caesar stone counter.

Northridge Remodel

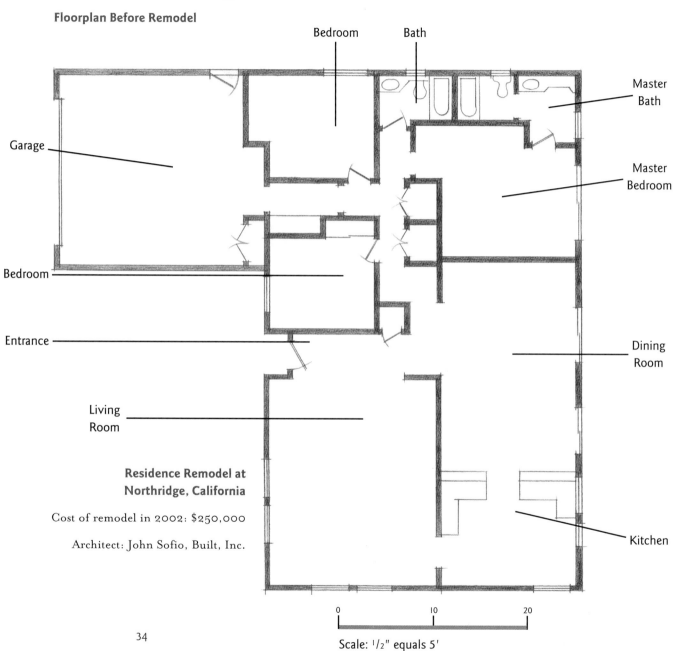

Floorplan Before Remodel

Bedroom

Bath

Master Bath

Garage

Master Bedroom

Bedroom

Entrance

Dining Room

Living Room

Residence Remodel at Northridge, California

Cost of remodel in 2002: $250,000

Architect: John Sofio, Built, Inc.

Kitchen

0   10   20

Scale: $^1\!/_2$" equals 5'

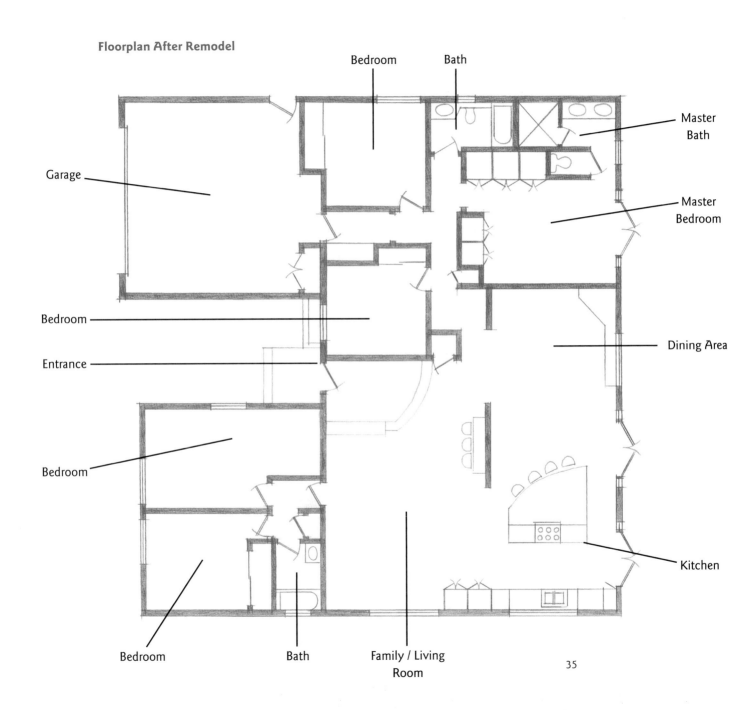

Floorplan After Remodel

Bedroom

Bath

Master Bath

Garage

Master Bedroom

Bedroom

Dining Area

Entrance

Bedroom

Kitchen

Bedroom

Bath

Family / Living Room

35

original floor plan to 2,500 square feet. The backyard pool was already in place but the patio was in poor shape and the overhangs were falling apart. Following the lines of the pool, Sofio installed a pergola to delineate a sitting area and shade the house, then built an outdoor dining court, complete with a cement-block barbecue station, beneath a new roof overhang. A strip of bluestone slate on the patio extends beyond the kitchen to "blur the line between inside and outside," he explains.

To brighten the interiors, Sofio added two shed dormers, rotating them for an unusual roofline effect. Other exterior fix-ups included sandblasting the existing Spanish lace textured stucco and replacing it with a smooth trowel finish stucco painted in understated shades of gray and green for a "Modernist Zen" appearance; replacing the cement shakes with long-lasting asphalt shingles; and adding depth and formality to the entry with a painted Douglas fir trellis, a

Like many slab-on-grade tract homes, this one had little visual impact.

The front entrance now has drama and depth thanks to the addition of a painted Douglas fir pergola, a cement-block fountain (to the left of the path), bluestone slate pavers, a vertical reed-glass panel (to the right of the door), and a two-step platform that introduces a height change and establishes a more pronounced sense of entry. Smooth-finish stucco gives the house a sophisticated appearance.

Although the pool was a plus, the challenge was to create a pleasant space around it.

An economical pergola constructed from painted Douglas fir framing material follows the lines of the pool and shades the side of the house and an outdoor sitting area. Douglas fir windows replaced the single-paned aluminum windows, and a redwood fence hides the pool equipment.

cement-block fountain, bluestone slate pavers, and a solid-core Douglas fir veneer door raised two steps to break up the monotony of the single-level elevation.

Inside, the house had predictable tract features—low, flat ceilings, blown-on textured drywall, and a floor plan of "dark, chunked-in non-spaces with poor circulation," Sofio says. Removing the ceilings and placing clerestory windows in the attic wall worked in tandem with the dormers to solve the problem of low light, and taking out interior walls brought a sense of flow to the main living zones. The home now has a variety of affordable materials, including ash veneer kitchen cabinets with a clear finish (less

Items of Interest:
The living room coffee table, bench seat, credenza, ottomans, and polka dot pillows are original designs by: John Sofio, Built, Inc.
323.857.0409
www.builtinc.com

The exposed beams and trusses are now a prominent design element. Above, dormer windows were popped into the roof and rotated at 22.5-degree angles for an eye-catching twist on typical dormer construction. To achieve this effect, the architect removed the low ceiling and cut into the plywood roof sheathing to make an opening for the dormers, which are supported by 2 x 6 rafters. Douglas fir French doors in an affordable off-the-shelf size replaced a 6-foot slider.

On the far left: The nonde-script kitchen before the remodel.

Low ceilings and small windows characterized the original living room.

The exterior entry platform continues beyond the front door with two curved steps made from poured concrete and overlain with black slate veneer to complement the bluestone slate veneer of the rest of the floors, previously covered in carpet. The slate is easy to clean and helps keep the interiors cool during the summer. The new ceiling, supported by 32-foot Douglas fir collar ties in a clear finish, is clad in affordable tongue-and-groove spruce painted white to match the smooth-finish drywall and medium-density fiberboard (MDF) baseboards and wood trim. The architect fashioned an inexpensive ($200) entry bench out of a glulam beam attached to the wall.

expensive than a stain); bluestone slate flooring; smooth-finish drywall; medium-density fiberboard (MDF) baseboards; Douglas fir windows and French doors in off-the-shelf sizes; Formica and Caesar stone counters; and Finlandian birch plywood.

Overall, Sofio focused this remodel on a series of middle-end solutions that adhered to the $100 per-square-foot budget and brought perhaps the most pleasing result: very happy clients.

Still in its original location but with a new high ceiling inset with a clerestory window, the bathroom received a major overhaul with stainless steel fixtures, a frameless glass shower enclosure, and a tile pattern in the shape of a waterfall. The cabinet is ribbon-grain mahogany veneer with a travertine counter.

A curved Finlandian birch plywood table topped with Formica and supported by a single chrome leg replaced a traditional kitchen table. Birch plywood is an economical choice because it doesn't require an edge band after being cut, which reduces labor. The table fits neatly against a counter with a Caesar stone top for a clean, casual look. Placing clerestory windows in the former attic took advantage of previously wasted space.

Blueprint #3

A 1960s tract is ushered into a new era with a renovation that speaks a contemporary language.

A Modern House in the Mountains

Aspen, Colorado

Cost of Remodel: $500,000 in 2000

Architect: Charles Bernstein, M. Charles Bernstein Architects

"Before" Photographs: Charles Bernstein

"After" Photographs: Robert Millman

Architect's Transformation Techniques:

—Preserve the existing foundation, structure, exterior wall cladding, and roofing to leave room in the budget for high-end detailing.

—Choose materials both for financial and design reasons, with the emphasis on a minimal palette of clear fir, maple, oxidized (rusted) sheet steel, and hand-rubbed galvanized sheet metal.

—Anchor the main level with a soffit that defines the open floor plan and orients the spaces toward the mountain views.

WHAT DO YOU do if you have an unexceptional house in an exceptional setting? Like many people who love where they live but are ready for a change in their living quarters, the owners of this Aspen home decided to stay put and work with what they had.

When the owners began discussions with architect Charles Bernstein, all agreed the house should not mimic the area's increasingly prevalent log aesthetic—in other words, it didn't need a log-intensive blueprint to be an authentic mountain dwelling. Not one to blindly follow trends, Bernstein had other ideas in mind for this project, which went on to win an American Institute of Architects Colorado

The architect worked with the home's existing form as much as possible, articulating new spaces from the structure in a way that minimized the footprint and reduced demolition costs. To square off the house and give it a contemporary appearance, he removed the roof overhangs and in several locations placed steel and spruce trellis overhangs for shade.

West Design Award for its fresh, contemporary look and thoughtful response to the site. "The remodel was meant to reflect residential architecture in a way that transcends the clichéd log cabin aesthetic," Bernstein explains. Indeed, this house has achieved a mountain vernacular without following the crowd.

Bernstein began the remodel by deciding which elements of the house could stay and which had to go. "It wasn't feasible to knock everything down and start over again," he explains. "Instead, we wanted to clearly express what is original and what is new." Preserving the foundation, wood siding, and roof met this goal (and brought significant savings), as did retaining key parts of the

The soffit support columns were in the original house but had been covered in drywall; the architect removed the drywall and acid-washed the columns to match the other steel features. The wall of windows was carefully arranged to maximally capture the views and allow natural light into the home.

Aspen Remodel

Main Level Plan After Remodeling

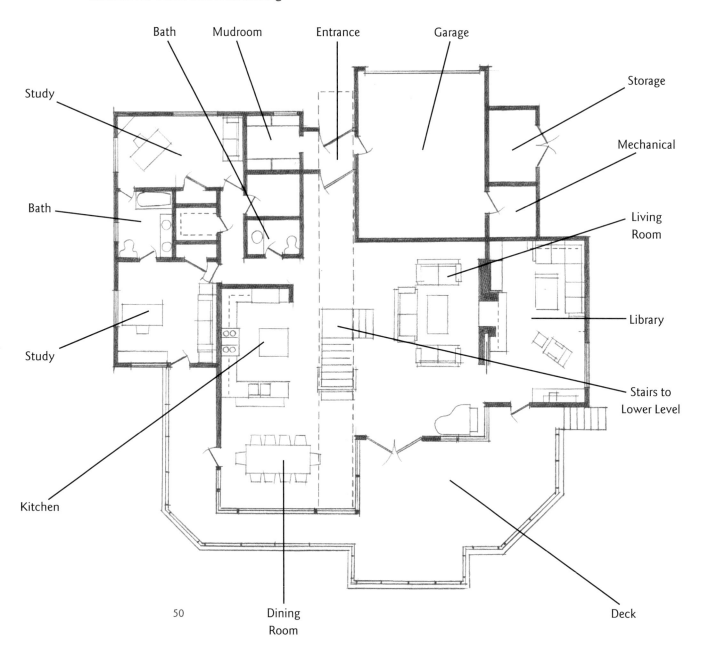

Study

Bath

Mudroom

Entrance

Garage

Storage

Mechanical

Study

Bath

Study

Living Room

Library

Stairs to Lower Level

Kitchen

Dining Room

Deck

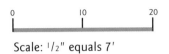

Scale: $^1/_2''$ equals 7'

Cost of Remodel in 2000: $500,000

Architect: Charles Bernstein,
M. Charles Bernstein Architects

South Elevation After Remodeling

Lower Level After Remodeling

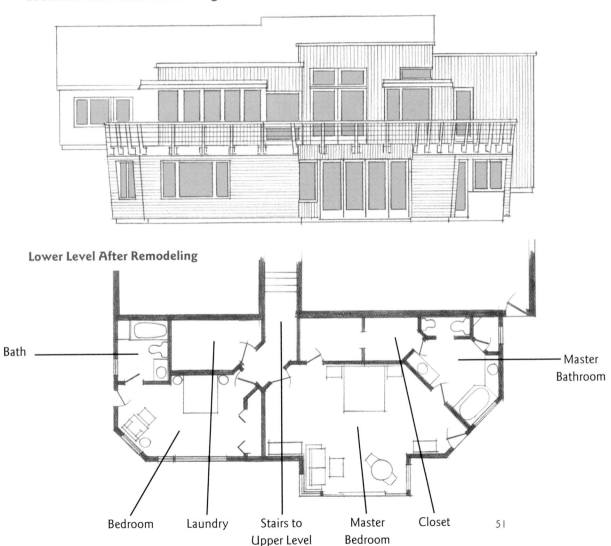

Bath

Master
Bathroom

Bedroom   Laundry   Stairs to
Upper Level   Master
Bedroom   Closet   51

To streamline the façade, the architect removed the eaves and disguised the existing wood siding with a spruce "pseudo-screen" that both refers to and moves away from the style of log architecture common to this and other mountain resort towns. To save money, the foundation and most of the exterior cladding and roofing were preserved.

52

Acid-washed copper siding at the entry provides a texture and color contrast to the spruce screen, which is set off from the wall so that it appears to float against the building. The new front door is wider than average (4.5 feet) and inset with frosted glass to soften the exterior. The steel canopy above the door extends from the interior soffit.

The home's desirable location made a remodel a wise investment.

building and articulating flat-roofed additions from them.

Bernstein also carefully studied the home's relationship to its site. Because the front faces the street, he kept it private and closed, disguising the existing wood siding with a heavy timber "pseudo-screen"—a technique that omitted the expense of new siding and established a downplayed reference to log construction while releasing the house from its tract heritage. The back faces the mountains, but the views had been hindered. To fix that problem, Bernstein conceived a dramatic wall of windows that frames the views and floods the house with natural light. After expanding the decks, he further embraced the views with a light, see-through railing.

Inside, Bernstein had to contend with a typical tract floor plan of small, separate rooms with poor lighting and routine finishes. The unraveling of the plan resulted in gutting and reconfiguring the entire central portion of the house to connect the living and dining rooms and kitchen. The next task was figuring out how to best take advantage of that open space and set the rooms off from each other now that their walls were gone. Bernstein's solution was twofold: he defined the living, dining, and kitchen areas with varying ceiling heights and anchored everything with a low-slung oxidized sheet steel soffit "spine" that runs the length of the house from the entrance to the window wall, strengthening the impact of the entry and leading the eye outward to the natural setting. Because the Aspen winters are long, Bernstein gave the rooms warmth with fir and maple and oxidized sheet steel, which, paired with "cooler" sheet metal, comprises the principal interior palette. Other interior alterations included widening the entry, adding a library/guest room, and converting two bedrooms into offices. Downstairs, the changes were limited to decorative revisions, leaving the bulk of the construction for the main floor—another way to trim costs.

The beauty of this tract house transformation lies both in its unique architectural expression and its practical, commonsense approach to remodeling. "The goal here was to combine old and new and in the process create richness while still keeping things simple," Bernstein says. "The house relates to its neighborhood, but it does so on its own terms."

Before

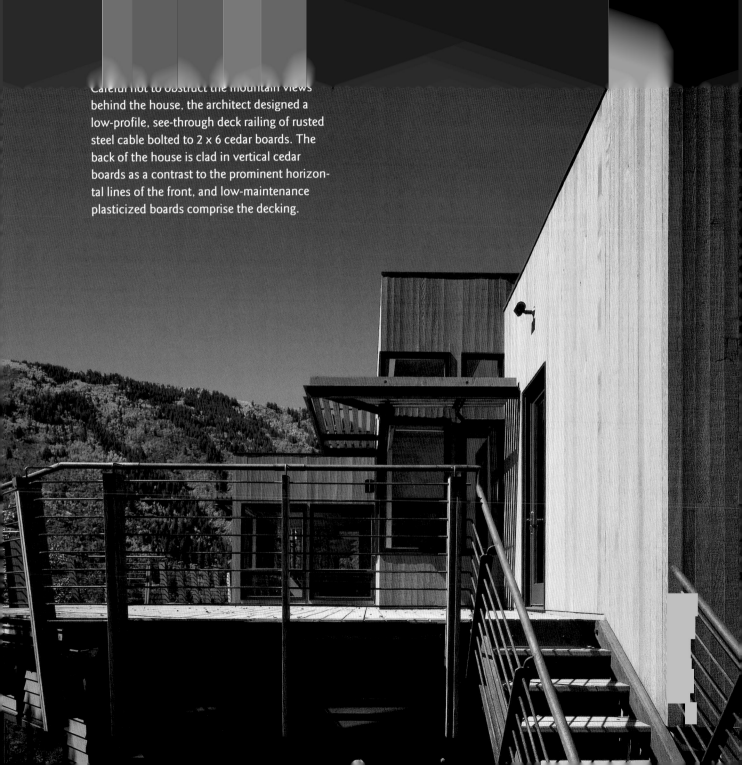

Careful not to obstruct the mountain views behind the house, the architect designed a low-profile, see-through deck railing of rusted steel cable bolted to 2 x 6 cedar boards. The back of the house is clad in vertical cedar boards as a contrast to the prominent horizontal lines of the front, and low-maintenance plasticized boards comprise the decking.

Previously narrow and dark, the hallway became an integral part of the remodeling plan.

Clear fir flooring, chosen for its warm tone, follows from the entry into the main living area. The dominant interior element and "spine" of the house is an oxidized sheet steel soffit, created with an acid wash and sealed with lacquer. The soffit runs the entire length of the house from the entrance to the south window wall, drawing the eye toward the view and imparting subtle divisions between the living room and kitchen/dining areas, originally separated by walls.

The stair, with its delicate railing, separates the
living room and kitchen. The architect worked with a
variety of ceiling heights to further define the spaces.

The oxidized sheet steel fireplace has a blued-steel hearth and a built-in maple television cabinet.

59

Expanding the kitchen by just three feet allowed for a 4 x 4 island that supplies additional storage and work surfaces. In keeping with the design scheme, the breakfast bar is a piece of rusted sheet steel bent and attached to the counter, and the backsplash is inexpensive hand-rubbed galvanized sheet metal. Maple cabinets and green granite counters bring color to the space.

Although spacious, the kitchen was bland.

A Philippe Starck sink rests between vertical panels of hand-rubbed galvanized sheet metal bonded to medium-density fiberboard (MDF) and sealed with lacquer. The recessed middle panel holds a mirror and a backlit glass shelf.

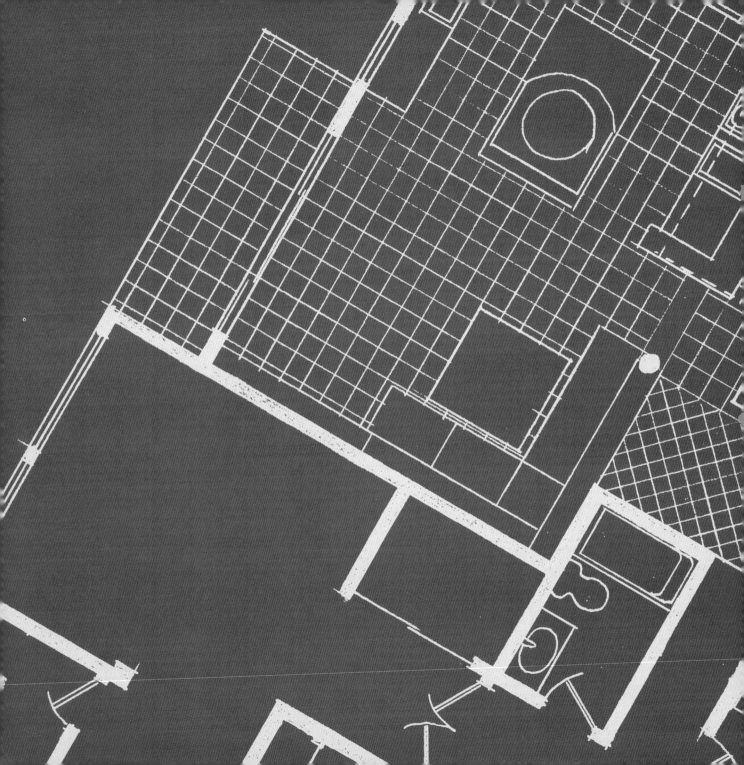

Blueprint #4

An exuberant bang–for–the–buck
remodel combines bold, playful
color with natural materials and
modern furnishings.

A House with a Case of the Blahs Gets a Winery-Inspired Facelift

Novato, California

Cost of Remodel: $220,000 in 2002

Architect: Mark English, Mark English Architects

"Before" Photographs: Mark English

"After" Photographs: Claudio Santini

Architect's Transformation Techniques:

—Work with the home's existing footprint and shell to cut costs and obey the parameters of the tiny lot.

—Emphasize the beauty of natural materials by using them in different applications for a refined expression that doesn't overwhelm the floor plan.

—Update the personality of the exterior with a colorful pool enclosure.

LOCATED IN SONOMA COUNTY in the heart of California wine country, this 1964 ranch-style tract house lacked distinction and character, but the owners had the vision—and patience—to see beyond its limitations. Both employed in the wine industry and enthusiastic cooks and party-givers, they wanted a house that would combine a winery aesthetic with the ambiance of a fine restaurant and feature bright color and a few whimsical touches here and there. After reviewing the work of San Francisco architect Mark English, they knew they had found a match. English, they discovered, could deliver the style they wanted—and he had a serious fun streak.

After twelve years in the house, the owners were ready to bid farewell to its painted plywood floors, dingy linoleum, low-ceilinged rooms, and uninspired interior scheme (imagine plain white walls—and more white walls). "The house was

Installed to help block traffic noise, the shotcrete fountain wall, painted an electric chartreuse, frames an 8-foot-long slate-clad trough that captures and circulates water.

65

mundane and poorly built, and to make things even more challenging, it occupies a tiny lot, so there wasn't room to expand," English says. "However, remodeling the house meant the owners could stay in the area. It was a better—and certainly more affordable—option than buying another house. In fact, this is one of the biggest bang-for-your-buck remodels my firm has done."

Due to the restrictions of the lot, the footprint of the 1,600-square-foot house didn't change. Instead, English worked with the basic shell, finding ways to reinvent rather than expand the existing spaces—a requirement that in turn kept the budget lean. The first major task was to remove most of the interior bearing walls in the kitchen, dining room, and living room to form one open space. (To further save money, the bedroom and bathroom walls were left intact.) After ripping out the ceiling boards and analyzing the structure, English found he was able to support the roof ridge with a single

Although the exterior did not change except for a new front door, the addition of a colorful pool/patio enclosure behind the house alludes to the updated interiors.

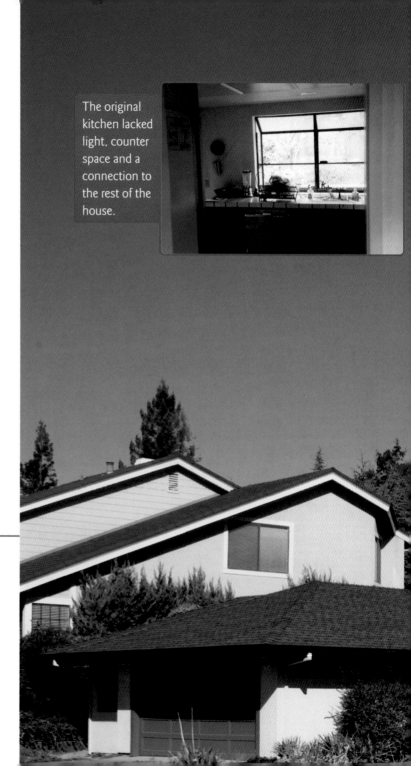

The original kitchen lacked light, counter space and a connection to the rest of the house.

The blocky, divided floor plan of the main living area is now a thing of the past.

The absence of color and texture gave the interiors a wan appearance.

Novato Remodel

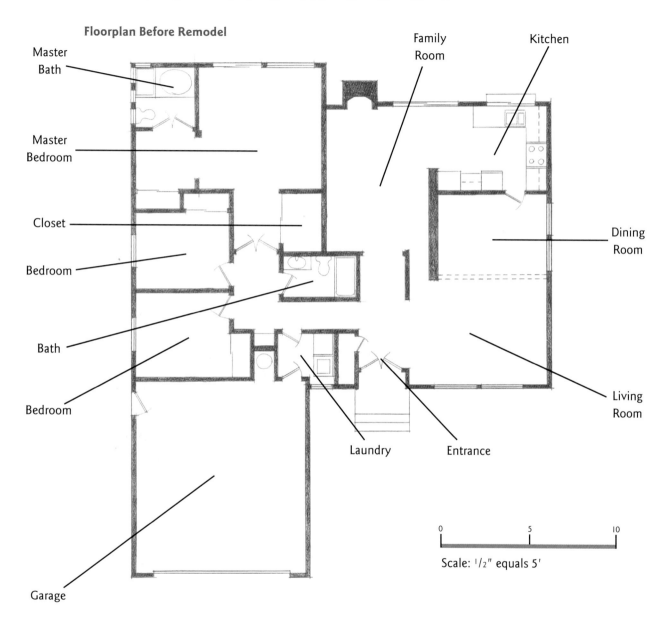

Floorplan Before Remodel

Master Bath

Family Room

Kitchen

Master Bedroom

Dining Room

Closet

Bedroom

Bath

Bedroom

Living Room

Laundry

Entrance

Garage

0   5   10

Scale: $^1/_2$" equals 5′

Floorplan After Remodel

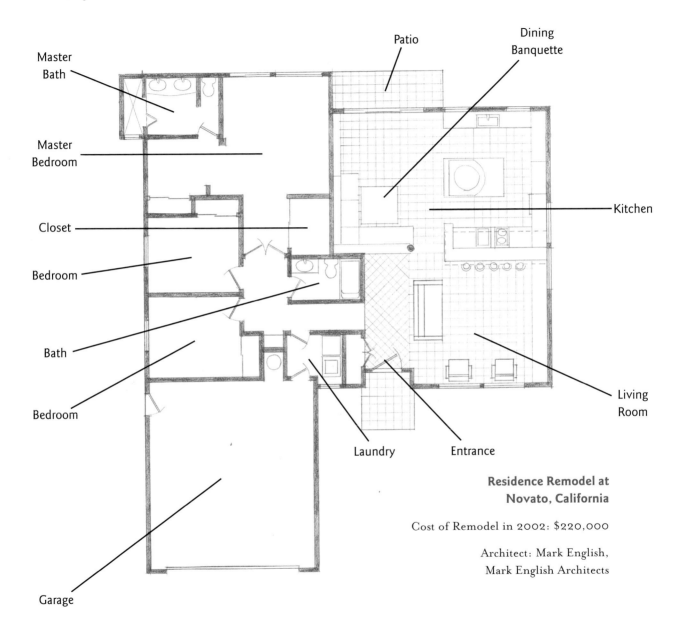

Patio

Dining Banquette

Master Bath

Master Bedroom

Kitchen

Closet

Bedroom

Bath

Living Room

Bedroom

Laundry

Entrance

Garage

Residence Remodel at Novato, California

Cost of Remodel in 2002: $220,000

Architect: Mark English, Mark English Architects

glulam beam, a technique that resulted in a delicately raised volume. Clerestory windows replaced a set of lower windows that had faced the street and a neighboring house, and larger windows in place of those in the living room were set closer to the floor for a more contemporary look.

The owners' love of cooking and entertaining made the kitchen a primary aspect of the remodel. "We thought carefully about what the kitchen should be," English says. "This was where we dealt with very specific needs." Today, the undisputed star of the kitchen is a large pizza oven, customized with a copper "wrapping" and Italian plaster cone vent. At 2,000 pounds, the oven needed a heavy-duty platform, and English chose a rustic base of flamed limestone. Although the oven itself was something of a splurge, English shaved dollars from the budget by tapping into his improvisational skills: rather than send out the smooth copper sheeting to an artisan for an expensive hammer finish, he placed it flat on the gravel driveway and instructed a construction worker to drive a truck over it to create the desired texture. (No wonder architects enjoy their work!)

In keeping with the goal of using natural materials, English selected two varieties of wood to establish what he describes as a "hierarchy of items throughout the space." For example, more everyday elements, such as the kitchen cabinets, are light-colored Eastern maple, while special features, such as the bar and the banquette, are crafted from natural cherry, which, with its darker hue and richer grain, beautifully complements the maple. Other interior

Modern designer furnishings contrast with the more rustic texture of the Chinese multicolored slate floor tiles and the nature-inspired hue of the pale green wall. New windows, set closer to the floor than the originals, give the room a bright, spacious feel.

Item of Interest:
The white living room chairs are by: Scylla
(information available through showrooms and interior designers)

materials include Chinese multicolored slate, stainless steel, and tinted cast concrete. Shortly after the indoor remodel was completed, the owners hired English to design a pool and outdoor dining patio. His response reveals both his love of color—in this case, chartreuse, raspberry, yellow and orange—and modernist sensibility.

Modestly, English believes the success of this transformation relied a great deal on the clients' willingness to experiment and enjoy the process. "These clients definitely have a good sense of humor," English says, "and, to an architect, that is always a bonus."

Item of Interest:
The light fixture over the dining table is by:
Translite Sonoma
707.966.6906
www.translitesonoma.com

In keeping with the home's informal personality, a built-in cherry banquette replaced the traditional dining room. The banquette, with its display shelves and storage drawers beneath the bench, forms a niche for the table, made from cherry and glass. To support the wall above the banquette, the architect installed a 4 x 4 structural column and clad it in authentic silver leaf. The wall facing the backyard reflects the chartreuse of the pool enclosure.

Overleaf:
High windows bring in daylight and maximize privacy, necessary in this closely knit neighborhood. Eastern maple kitchen cabinets complement the cherry bar, which is topped with a cast-concrete counter tinted gray-green. The small floor plan responded well to built-ins and streamlined cabinetry, which do not intrude into the already limited space.

Item of Interest:
The "Spica" dining room chairs are by:
Montis
For information and dealer locations: www.montis.nl

The pizza oven, with its Italian plaster cone vent, textured copper (created by driving a truck over a smooth sheet of copper placed on the gravel driveway), cast-concrete counter, and flamed limestone base, is the focal point of the kitchen. The steel-and-brick prefabricated oven arrives from the manufacturer as a basic unit that can then be "wrapped" as desired.

Designed by the architect, the glass canopy suspended above the bar provides a sense of separation between the kitchen and living room and balances the height of the ceiling volume. Constructed of panels of ruled glass set into a steel frame finished with a clear lacquer, the canopy is lit from above by recessed low-volt lights that shine down on the rippling glass, creating a glowing effect that is especially dramatic at night.

The new bathroom has a —————————————————
Calicatta Gold marble counter,
cherry cabinets, chrome
towel bars, 2 x 2 porcelain
tiles, and 18-inch squares of
Chinese multicolored slate
floor tiles. A pull-out hamper
sits below the counter for
easy access. As in the dining
room, the wall reflects the
color of the pool enclosure.

Alvin, purportedly the true owner of
the house, enjoys easy indoor-outdoor
access thanks to a custom doggie door
built into a nook at the end of a kitchen
cabinet. It's a dog's life!

The exuberant pool enclosure features
a wall in a shade of raspberry and
Plexiglas panels set into a wood frame.

A painted shotcrete wall and row of cement blocks form the perimeter of the pool, which is lined in simple white tiles.

An informal poolside dining table is shaded by a steel structure inset with a rectangular sheet of steel tubing. The retaining wall and bench are Brazilian redwood.

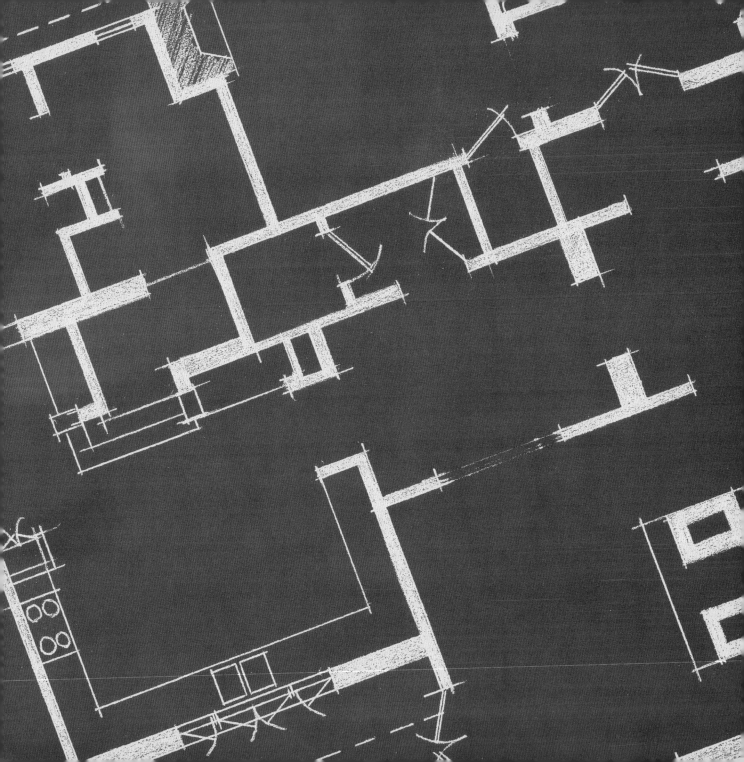

Blueprint #5

A custom home emerges from a 1950s tract, proving that humble beginnings can lead to spectacular results.

Tuscany Comes to Texas

Cost of Remodel: $575,000 in 2002

Architect: Hugh Jefferson Randolph

All Photographs: Hugh Randolph

Architect's Transformation Techniques:

—Minimize the number of new two-story walls to prevent the house from overpowering its one-story neighbors.

—Rework the disjointed floor plan around a centralized axis to improve transitions between rooms.

—Use understated, durable materials, including integral-color stucco, copper, and locally quarried limestone.

THANKS TO A SPIRITED creative alliance between architect and client and a healthy budget, this 1950s ranch has metamorphosed into a slice of Tuscany in Austin. The owners had rented the home before deciding to buy it—more for its established neighborhood and quick commute to downtown than its architectural pizzazz. "This is a very desirable area," explains architect Hugh Randolph, "and the clients realized that the value of the market could support a remodel of this scope."

Because the house was destined for a significant renovation—not quite a tear-down but more extensive than a straightforward remodel—Randolph took pains to ensure it would be "friendly rather than overbearing and still fit in the neighborhood." This was accomplished by

With its unusual scale (its vaulted ceiling makes it taller than it is wide), oversized fireplace, and narrow windows divided by strips of flat Sheetrock to match the untrimmed walls, the dining room was the most dramatic change in the house. Antique long-leaf pine floors add warmth and rusticity to the elegant room.

Like other tract houses built in Austin during the 1950s, this one was constructed with materials meant to give it an historic appearance.

The house, with its modified Tuscan façade, is now a combination of straightforward forms and subtle materials such as stucco and copper. The architect was careful to limit the number of two-story walls on the addition so the building would not overpower its one-story neighbors. The home office in the one-story wing to the right has a separate entrance with a landscaped terrace.

Austin Remodel

Main Level After Remodel

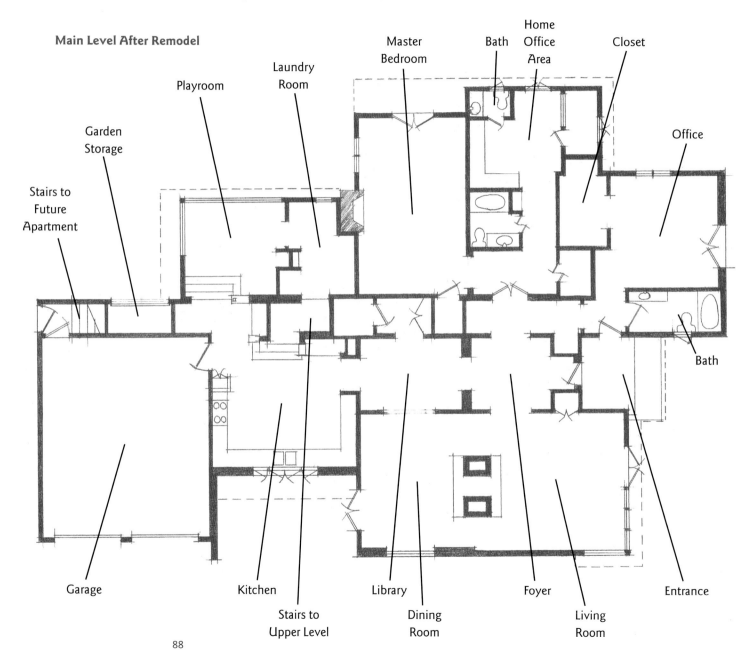

Garden
Storage

Playroom

Laundry
Room

Master
Bedroom

Bath

Home
Office
Area

Closet

Office

Stairs to
Future
Apartment

Bath

Garage

Kitchen

Stairs to
Upper Level

Library

Dining
Room

Foyer

Living
Room

Entrance

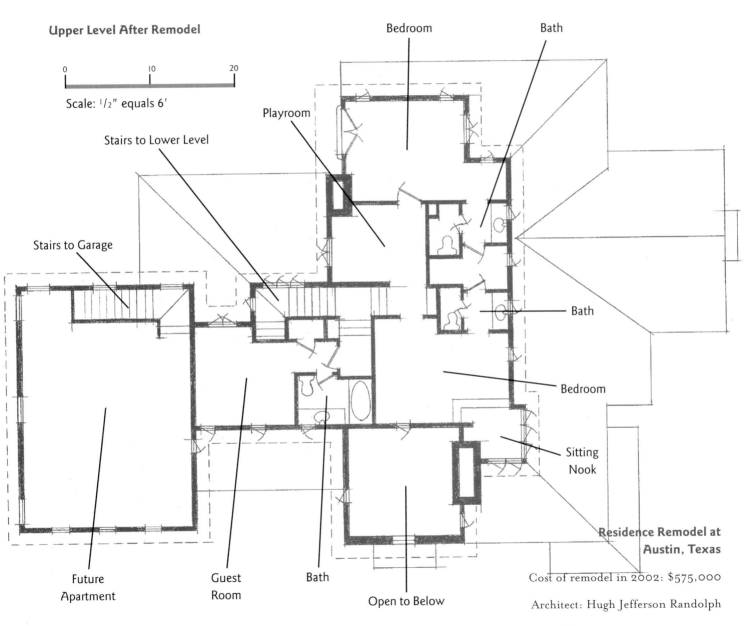

Upper Level After Remodel

0   10   20

Scale: 1/2" equals 6'

Stairs to Lower Level

Playroom

Bedroom

Bath

Stairs to Garage

Bath

Bedroom

Sitting Nook

Future Apartment

Guest Room

Bath

Open to Below

Residence Remodel at Austin, Texas

Cost of remodel in 2002: $575,000

Architect: Hugh Jefferson Randolph

keeping the number of two-story walls on the addition to a minimum and using a limited palette of downplayed exterior materials accented by quiet details. Although many sections of the house had to be demolished due to wood rot, those that could be saved helped influence the new footprint. After plenty of discussion and exchange of ideas with Randolph, the owners wrote a wish list that included a more spacious living room and kitchen, a home office with its own entry, an outdoor dining patio, a playroom, and updated children's rooms. The

Painted wood French doors, shaded by a copper awning, allow natural light into the living room and connect the interiors to the garden.

A number of discreet exterior details, such as this delicate steel bracket, express the pride and care of the owners.

Varying roof planes and wall heights create a home that, while large, has excellent proportion. Made from Texas Lueders limestone blocks, the chimney provides texture against the smooth stucco and is the transition between the building's short and tall volumes.

architect responded with a design that defines private and public spaces and doesn't dominate the site or the neighbors.

To break up the massing of the two-story house, Randolph alternated wall heights and combined different roof angles to give the 4,200-square-foot home the appearance of having evolved over time. Other large-scale changes involved moving the master bedroom to the old living room for a more private setting, relocating the garage to allow for the expansion of the kitchen, turning the screened porch into a playroom, placing children's bedrooms on the second floor, developing the living and dining areas, and creating a courtyard with an outdoor dining patio. A one-story wing on the front of the house accommodates a home office with a landscaped terrace and separate entrance, making it possible for the owner to keep her work and home life distinct.

The exterior of the house reveals focal elements "meant to instill interest and produce a sculptural effect," Randolph says. The top roof ridge ties the building together and complements the varying angles of the lower roof planes, while the recessed front door is framed by an arched entry that anchors the façade. Integral-color stucco contributes to the home's Tuscan charm and is a neutral backdrop for copper awnings, a limestone chimney, and decorative steel awning brackets. Inside, materials run the gamut from basic

A copper awning shades the courtyard, visible from inside the kitchen through wood windows painted to match the French doors at the front of the house. The arrangement of spaces and close indoor/outdoor relationship is reminiscent of an Italian farmhouse.

The screened porch was transformed into a sunny playroom.

93

Sheetrock to antique long-leaf pine floors, a limestone fireplace, wood French doors, and granite.

For Randolph, this project was about more than simply remodeling a house. "The architect-client relationship is important and key to a successful outcome," he says. "It's crucial for the architect to discover the clients' bigger goals and guide them through the process of arriving at the house they want. It's like a puzzle—you look at what the client wants and then figure out how to make it all fit together."

The house was in poor shape and suffered from wood rot, discovered in the living room and elsewhere during construction.

The fireplace divides the dining and living rooms. The dining room side, shown here, reveals an artistic juxtaposition of locally quarried Texas limestone and a mosaic pattern of tan, yellow, and gold-colored glass tiles.

Relocated to the original site of the master bedroom, the living room is casual and low-key. French doors painted white complement the Sheetrock walls, kept free of trim to give the illusion of stucco or plaster.

The kitchen remained in the same place but was expanded, with new appliances and windows that open to the courtyard. The maple butcher-block island was designed to look like a piece of furniture, and the color palette was kept simple with off-white paint-grade wood cabinets and glazed-finish tiles and gray honed-granite counters.

Item of Interest:
The kitchen range is by:
Thermador
800.656.9226
www.thermador.com

To fix the disjointed floor plan, the architect focused the rooms around a centralized axis that follows from the foyer through a sitting-room/library and back to the kitchen. The inside arches mimic the arched front entry for continuity between the exterior and interior. The floors are antique long-leaf pine here and throughout the house.

Item of Interest:
The hanging silk lamp in the foyer is by:
Mariano Fortuny
212.753.7153
For information:
www.fortuny.com

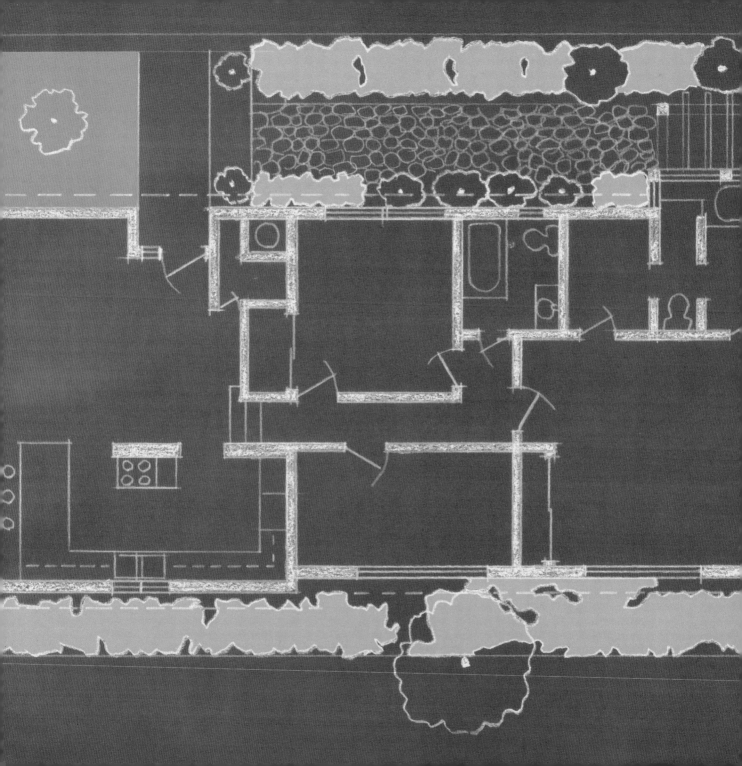

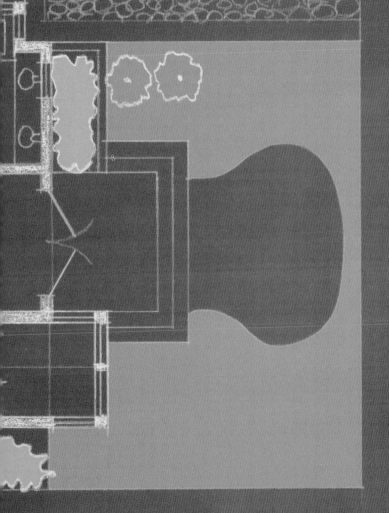

Blueprint #6

An innovative solution turns a fixer-upper bungalow into a home perfectly suited to a young family.

Trading Spaces

Cost of Remodel: $150,000 in 1997

Architect: Grant Kirkpatrick, Kirkpatrick Associates Architects

"Before" Photographs: Courtesy of architect

"After" Photographs: Weldon Brewster

Architect's Transformation Techniques:

—Flip the floor plan, moving the main living spaces to the back of the house and placing an expanded master suite at the front.

—Shift the entry to the side of the house and turn the driveway into a landscaped path that leads to a dining court and fenced-in yard.

—Choose materials for affordability and durability, including vinyl composite floors, limestone, paint-grade medium-density fiberboard (MDF), and Douglas fir.

The house glows at night thanks to wide French doors and clerestory windows in the office nook and master bathroom.

To GRANT AND SHAYA KIRKPATRICK, this bungalow-style tract house in Manhattan Beach had plenty going for it—an attractive setting a quick drive to their offices in Los Angeles, excellent schools, and an eclectic population. The house itself, though, had a few significant drawbacks, namely what struck them as a backwards floor plan. "The house was a good buy, and we believed we could improve it and bring it up to speed," Grant Kirkpatrick says. "We could see that it had wonderful potential."

Like many houses of its time, the home's street-side entrance opened directly into the living and dining area and a kitchen that had been squeezed into a corner. From there followed bedrooms and a family room in the back that faced the garage, accessed by a driveway running parallel to the house. Tapping into their talents (Grant is an architect and Shaya an interior designer), the couple devised a clever solution: they rotated the floor plan 180 degrees in a rearrangement tailored to their lifestyle. One of the key goals was to create a safe outdoor area for their children. "We needed a protected place for the kids to play outside," Grant explains, "one that could be supervised, if necessary, from inside the house."

A glulam beam along the roof ridge supports the ceiling where walls once stood and has been painted white to match the tongue-and-groove cladding and purlins. Although it resembles mahogany, the flooring is a vinyl composite wood that is "virtually indestructible," according to the architect, making it a smart choice for families with children or pets. The kitchen counters are German Green Stone, a type of limestone, and the fireplace, still with its original green slate hearth, has been modernized with a smooth trowel finish plaster surround. Large glazed doors lead to the yard and make it possible to supervise children at play outside from any point in the room.

Manhattan Beach Remodel

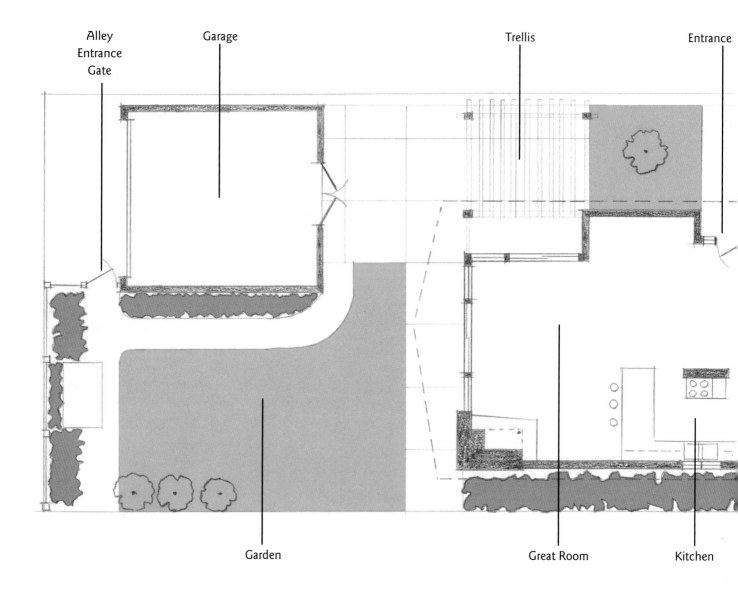

Alley
Entrance
Gate

Garage

Trellis

Entrance

Garden

Great Room

Kitchen

0   5   10   15   20

Scale: $^1/_2$" equals 5'

Floorplan After Remodel

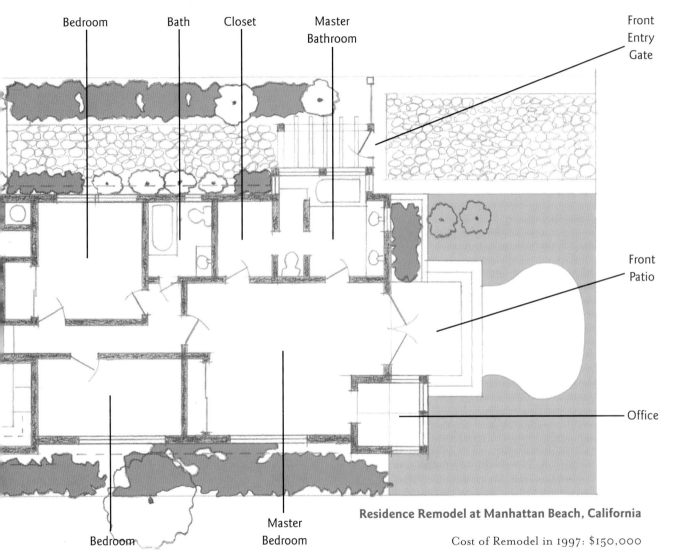

Bedroom   Bath   Closet   Master Bathroom

Front Entry Gate

Front Patio

Office

Bedroom

Master Bedroom

Residence Remodel at Manhattan Beach, California

Cost of Remodel in 1997: $150,000

Architect: Grant Kirkpatrick, Kirkpatrick Associates Architects

Not only did the 1940s bungalow lack architectural interest, its driveway took up outdoor space that could be put to better use. Inside, the family room had an uninspiring view of the garage, and the kitchen was crowded into a corner just beyond the front door.

Floorplan Before Remodel

Garage

Driveway

Garden

Family Room

Bath

Bed

Bath

Kitchen

Bed

Bed

Living Room

Floorplan After Remodel

Garage

Pergola

Garden

Entrance

Great Room

Kitchen

Bed

Bath

Bed

Master Bath

Master Bed

Office

The entry was shifted to the side of the house to claim the space occupied by the driveway. The new "front" door is accessed through a gate made from 2 x 4 painted tube steel and translucent laminate glass panels, which opens to a landscaped side yard and path. The exterior was refurbished with board-and-batten siding in the gable and smooth trowel finish plaster on the office and master bathroom popouts; the existing brick was painted white to keep the house within the context of the neighborhood. Standard paint-grade Douglas fir windows and French doors give the home a contemporary façade.

The flip was straightforward: the living/dining room and kitchen at the front were turned into a master suite with a small adjacent office, formed by enclosing the stoop. The original master bedroom is now the kitchen, part of a multifunctional great room in the back that encompasses a living and dining area. The two center bedrooms were left intact. By adhering to the footprint and adding just 100 square feet in the form of pop-outs in the walls of the office, master bathroom, and dining section of the great room, the Kirkpatricks were able to minimize construction on the shell of the house, which in turn saved them money.

With the master bedroom now at the front, the entry had to be relocated. Realizing that the driveway was consuming precious space, the Kirkpatricks turned it into a landscaped path and shifted the main entrance to the side of the house. The path passes by the entry on its way to a dining patio sheltered by a pergola and a yard surrounded by a privacy fence. In yet another resourceful move, the Kirkpatricks transferred the garage

access to the alley side of the lot and placed French doors in the original door opening to disguise the building.

Although only 1,650 square feet, the home seems larger, an effect enhanced by the open great room and a vaulted ceiling supported by a glulam beam. The beam made it possible to remove walls, a technique Grant believes is fundamental to remodeling smaller homes. "There is always one wall that can be taken out and in doing so make all the difference in the world," he explains. "In this case, it allowed the house to start breathing." Sizable glass doors contribute to this spaciousness and, if the kids are outside, offer unobstructed views to them from any point in the great room.

Interior materials were chosen both for their appearance and durability and include a vinyl composite floor that resembles mahogany, limestone, medium-density fiberboard, and painted Sheetrock. "The best thing about the house is its easy living," says Grant, "and what is now a real flow between the indoors and outdoors."

Previously the location of the driveway, the side yard is now an inviting path landscaped with tufted grasses, rosemary, lavender, and Mexican sage. The path passes by the relocated entry and ends at a dining court and patio surrounded by a privacy fence. The garage entrance was moved to the alley behind the property, and the original opening was replaced with French doors.

Overleaf:

Keeping materials to a minimum saved money and gave the home a casual, easygoing charm. The functional kitchen includes a breakfast bar and flush-panel medium-density fiberboard (MDF) cabinets complemented by a white tongue-and-groove ceiling and walls in a lively shade of yellow. Built-in shelves neatly store books and CDs.

To add a recycled element to the house, the architect broke up the concrete driveway and used the pieces as flagstones to line the walkway.

Constructed of standard framing lumber, the pergola shades the courtyard and provides a visual and physical link between the indoor and outdoor spaces. The architect replaced the solid wall with a glass door, flanked by tall windows and topped with transom lights, for easy access to the dining area.

Previously the site of the living/dining room and kitchen, the street side of the house is now a master suite with a full bath and walk-in closet. The stoop was turned into a small office by extending the front wall 5 feet to make it flush with the bottom step and then enclosing the space with a smooth trowel finish plaster box capped with a peaked roof inset with clerestory windows. French doors open to a raised patio off the suite; the patio is painted 2 x 6 standard-grade redwood.

Formerly the kitchen, the master bathroom features limestone tiles on the counters, tub surface, and floors. Bumping out a portion of the wall made room for a whirlpool tub and walk-in shower and was a cost-effective alternative to a more extensive expansion. The cabinets are affordable flush-panel medium-density fiberboard (MDF), and clerestory windows bring in light without compromising privacy.

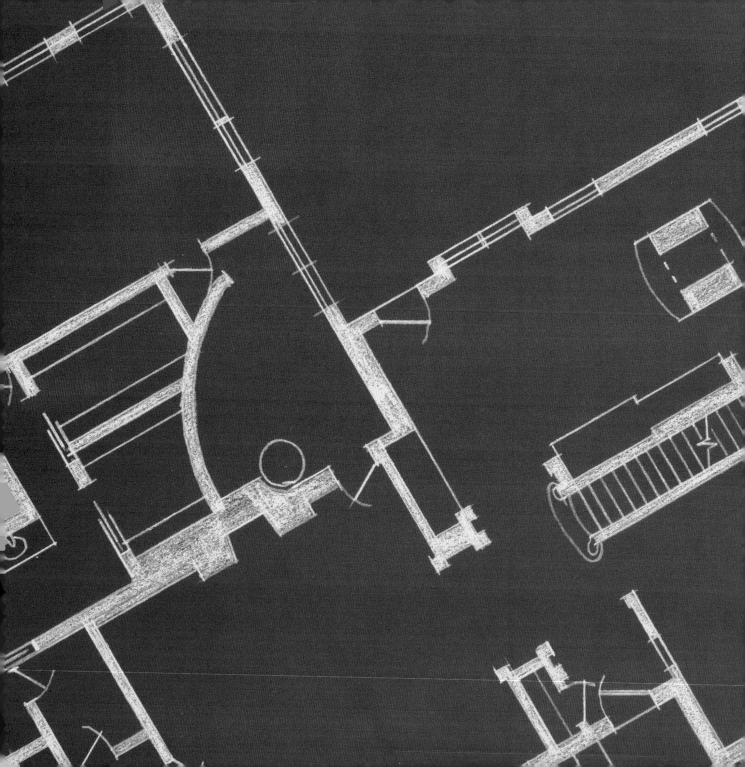

Blueprint #7

An Arts and Crafts–inspired family home rises from a mediocre but well-maintained 1950s ranch.

Commonplace to Custom

Cost of Remodel: $450,000 in 2001

Architects: Fred Wilson and Elissa Morgante, Morgante Wilson Architects

"Before" Photographs: Courtesy of architects

"After" Photographs: Elissa Morgante (exterior) and Hilary Rose (interior)

Architects' Transformation Techniques:

—Adhere to the footprint and add a second story for children's bedrooms and to break up the flatness of the façade.

—Modify the fragmented floor plan into one with a flexible, open layout that easily accommodates family life and entertaining.

—Incorporate Arts and Crafts–style elements for a warm, inviting look inside and out.

IF YOU HAD SEEN this house prior to its transformation, you might not recognize it now. Before the remodel, it was a humdrum ranch similar in appearance to countless others, with a floor plan that was "deceptively small because of the way it was arranged," says architect Fred Wilson. Today, it is a welcoming and functional family-oriented home that has gracefully shed its tract constraints—with results that are nothing less than head-turning.

Having previously designed a number of tract remodels, Wilson and his partner Elissa Morgante were well-versed in the ways this house could be improved. "Early tract developers figured out how to cut corners and build these homes as cheaply as possible," Morgante explains. "But, although they lack compelling features and need greater thought put into

The stair landing overlooks the tall entry hall and has a slim rail for an open, airy effect. Arches here and elsewhere in the house refer to the Arts and Crafts motif, and the dining room's leaded-glass window imparts a sense of transparency to the entrance.

their layouts, they are often in nice areas and people are willing to spend the money to fix them up, as was the case here."

Built in the late 1950s, this house had enough desirable qualities—a good neighborhood in the Chicago suburbs, sturdy construction, and consistent maintenance over the years—to make a remodel worthwhile. Taking into account both the home's drawbacks and its untapped potential, Wilson and Morgante, working closely with project managers Susan Patenaud and Jeff Gruska, directed a makeover that emphasizes livable spaces for this family of five and a decorative theme that focuses on materials and stylistic elements borrowed from the Arts and Crafts movement. "Flexibility was very important for this client," Wilson explains, "as was a home that was comfortable and inviting."

—Although the house had received plenty of TLC over the years, its one-level layout did not suit the current owners' needs.

Unrecognizable in its transformed state, the home now has distinctive —— Arts and Crafts detailing and a new second story that helps break up the flatness of the façade and accommodates children's bedrooms. The architects added a stone pillar to mark the driveway, pulled the garage out and forward to make space for the addition, and replaced the roofing with long-lasting asphalt shingles.

Chicago Remodel

Main Level After Remodel

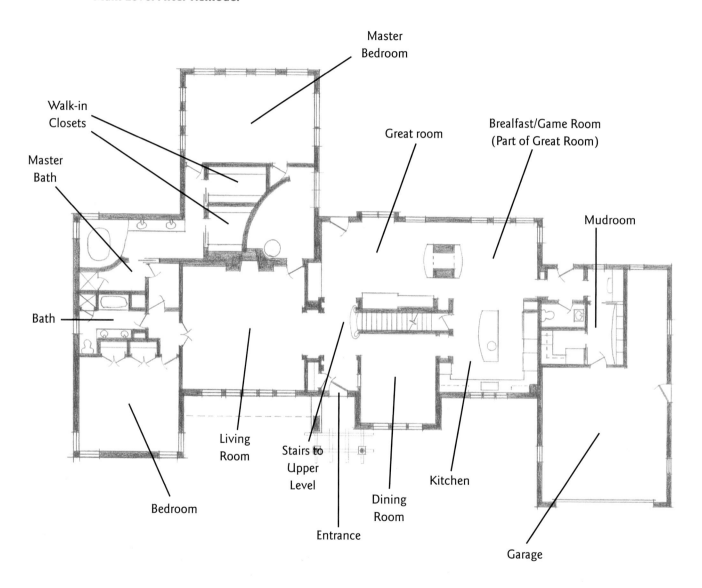

Master Bedroom

Walk-in Closets

Master Bath

Bath

Great room

Brealfast/Game Room (Part of Great Room)

Mudroom

Bedroom

Living Room

Stairs to Upper Level

Entrance

Dining Room

Kitchen

Garage

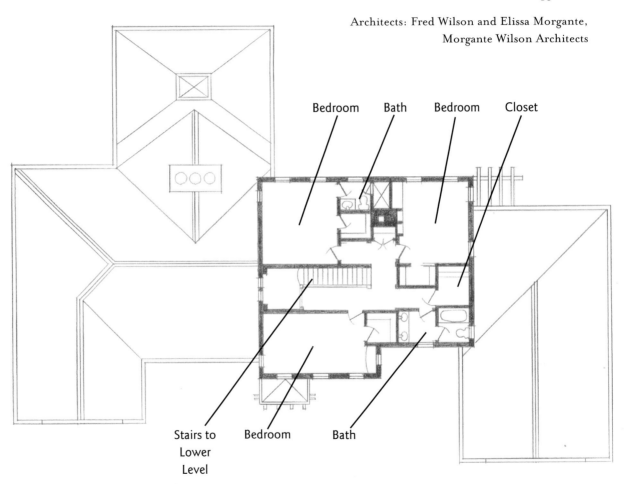

Bedroom   Bath   Bedroom   Closet

Stairs to
Lower
Level

Bedroom   Bath

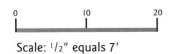

0   10   20

Scale: $^{1}/_{2}''$ equals 7'

Without expanding the original footprint, the owners wanted to provide individual bedrooms for their children. The architects' solution was to add a second story with three bedrooms and two bathrooms. This configuration of rooms in turn gave the adults privacy, as they decided to stay in the first-floor master suite.

Heeding the owners' request for a practical floor plan that worked with their lifestyle, the architects turned the back bedrooms into a great room with a double-sided fireplace that separates the entertainment area from the breakfast/game room, and opened the enclosed kitchen to the great room. The family room was converted into an informal everyday entry that leads into a mudroom with built-in storage cubbies and cabinets, and then on to a laundry room, small office, and powder

Assembled off-site for savings, the stair is an elegant combination of oak (treads, trim, and rail) and painted wood risers and round newel posts. The simple walls and trim provide a backdrop for the more textural elements of the home.

The original one-level section of the house is visible to the left of the entry, which leads into the two-story addition. The façade was updated with a mahogany door, a wood entry canopy with a copper roof and Arts and Crafts–style brackets, and painted wood casement and double-hung windows. The existing stone base was extended up to the second story windowsills.

room. The interior materials palette includes oak floors with walnut inlays, cherry cabinetry, leaded glass, granite, ceramic tile, and slate.

Although raising ceilings is a popular technique in many tract remodels, Wilson and Morgante felt that keeping them low would complement and enhance the Arts and Crafts motif. Nonetheless, the plain Sheetrock in the living room clearly lacked visual interest and depth, which the architects solved with a grid of painted wood beams and recessed lighting. The height was saved for the entry hall, which reaches to the second floor, creating space for a dignified stair and bringing a sense of drama to this public part of the house. "The entry hall is meant to be open and light,"

Morgante says. "And, it balances the other rooms, which are more intimate in scale."

Outside, the recessed front door sits beneath an arched entry canopy with bracket accents and a copper roof, and the stone base extends up to the second-floor windowsills for consistency in detailing and to help ground the building. Casement and double-hung mullioned wood windows in a variety of sizes allow light inside and "provide a great deal of dimension to the house," Wilson points out, adding, "These houses are really not that difficult to transform. With some creativity and effort, you can take a boring one-story ranch, add a second story like we did with this project, and give it so much more character."

The kitchen before.

Overleaf:

The relocated and expanded kitchen is both functional and inviting thanks to ample granite work surfaces, stainless steel appliances, cherry cabinets with leaded-glass doors, ceramic tiles, and oak floors.

A Sheetrock arch implies a transition between the kitchen and breakfast room without the need for a door. The island doubles as a sink and prep counter.

The living room's dimensions did not change, but the introduction of warm, earthy materials and a traditional décor gave it an Arts and Crafts appearance. To alleviate the monotony of the Sheetrock ceiling, which was kept low to enhance the intimacy of the room, the architects installed painted wood beams and recessed lighting. The oak floor is accented with a walnut inlay for an eye-catching way to delineate the room from the others.

The best thing about the original living room was its spaciousness.

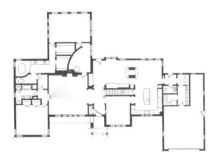

The mudroom features a durable, low-maintenance slate floor and a wall of built-in cubbies and cupboards for neatly storing sports gear, coats, and other items. The cubbies are crafted from low-cost beaded board and the cabinets and bench are cherry.

The mudroom leads to a small home office.

The dining room had been hemmed in by walls.

The dining room "paneling" is 1 x 4 trim material applied
to the wall in a clever technique that is less expensive
than true wood paneling. The leaded-glass window
sends soft light from the entry hall into the room.

133

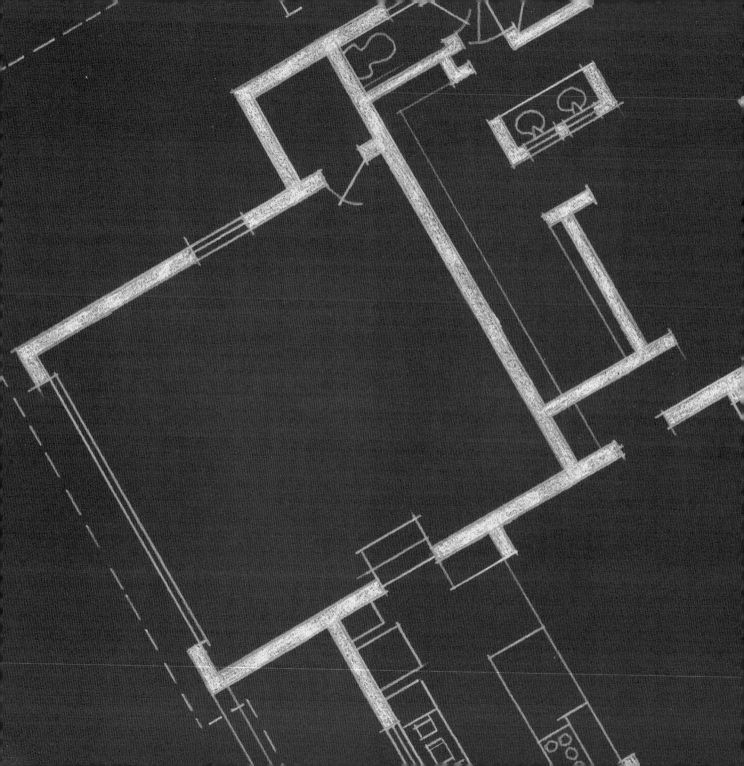

Blueprint #8

An environmentally sensitive and budget-conscious remodel reveals the hidden beauty of a Bay Area tract.

From Just Like the Others To One-of-a-Kind

San Mateo, California

Architects: David Arkin and Anni Tilt,
Arkin Tilt Architects

"Before" Photographs: Courtesy of the architects

"After" Photographs: Edward Caldwell

Architects' Transformation Techniques:

—Use the path of the Sun to orient the floor plan to bring natural light into the spaces and reduce energy consumption.

—Incorporate sustainable and salvaged materials to save money and meet the goal of an eco-friendly house.

—With minimal expansion, reconfigure the existing square footage into a more practical arrangement of rooms that better suits the owners' lifestyle.

"OFTEN REMODELS REPRESENT missed opportunities," says David Arkin of Berkeley-based Arkin Tilt Architects. "Many people think of them as adding and covering and don't realize they can reveal the bones of the building and take that authenticity and express it beautifully."

Built as part of a development outside San Francisco, this 1959 ranch looked like every other house on the block. But, as Anni Tilt explains, "Typical of this era, the building had very good bones—it just wasn't altogether thoughtfully designed. Our job was to discover the possibilities of the lovely site and integrate the structure and square footage into new rooms that worked for this family."

Added in the 1960s, the red stucco portion of the house was a family room until a simple rearrangement—switching the family room and master bedroom—turned it into a master suite now expanded by 168 square feet. The architects modernized this corner of the house with a new hip roof wrapped around the flat roof, a trellis supported by a madrone tree column, and clerestory windows. The "bleacher seat" deck was built from existing planks of redwood saved during construction.

137

Admirable construction aside, the house was a study in the all-too-common faults of the tract house: small, insufficiently lit rooms, low ceilings, tight circulation, and what the architects describe as "utter disregard for solar orientation and connection to the site." The remodel began with an analysis of the interior and exterior spaces, followed by a rearrangement of functions within the existing plan. The family room, located in a flat-roofed addition built in the 1960s, was expanded into a master bedroom suite, the family room was moved to where the master bedroom had been, and the dining room was turned into a bedroom, forming a suite of rooms known as the Girls' Wing. To create a great room, the architects removed the walls

The expanded deck, with its open railing and stepped-down levels, strengthens the relationship of the house to its site and allows for uninterrupted canyon views. Bold colors and a more visually engaging roofline give the house a contemporary appearance.

San Mateo Remodel

Floorplan Before Remodel

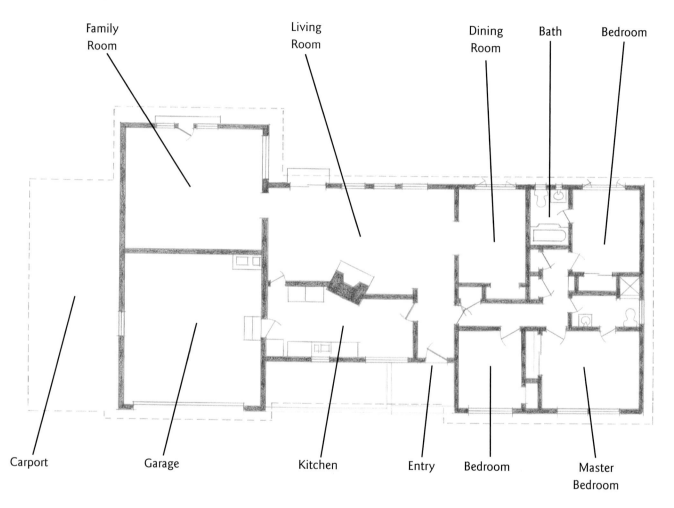

Family Room

Living Room

Dining Room

Bath

Bedroom

Carport

Garage

Kitchen

Entry

Bedroom

Master Bedroom

Scale: $^1/_2$" equals 7'

Floorplan After Remodel

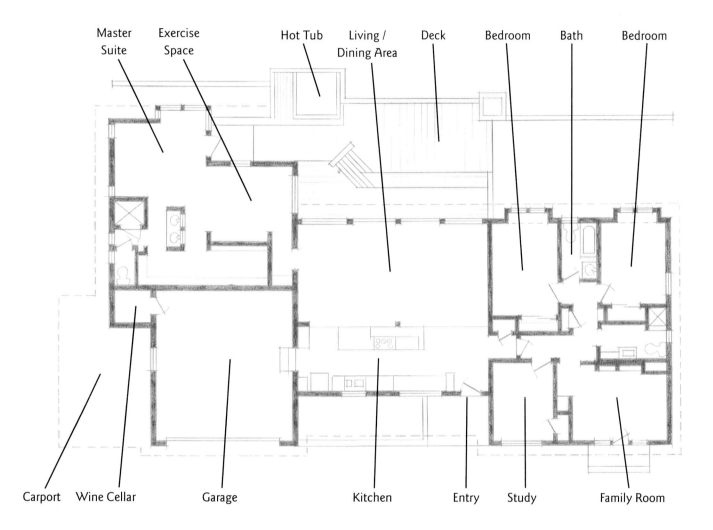

Master Suite · Exercise Space · Hot Tub · Living / Dining Area · Deck · Bedroom · Bath · Bedroom

Carport · Wine Cellar · Garage · Kitchen · Entry · Study · Family Room

Residence Remodel at San Mateo, California

Cost of remodel: withheld

Architects: David Arkin and Anni Tilt, Arkin Tilt Architects

and brick fireplace that had divided the kitchen, living room, and entry and installed wide glass doors on barn sliders to open the room to the deck. The house, completed in 2000, is now a modest but livable 2,094 square feet.

Arkin and Tilt also paid close attention to how natural light could be brought into and shared between rooms. They even went so far as to test a scale model of the house on a heliodon, a device that simulates the sun's path on any day of the year, and used the data to maximize daylighting inside. The result of this scientific approach is a cupola on the south side of the roof ridge, in the attic volume previously hidden by a ceiling. In the summer, the cupola ventilates and cools

The front of the house was essentially unchanged and only hints at the remodel from the street, most notably in the cupola that rises from the roof.

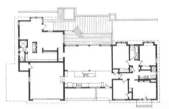

The house was similar to others on the street.

142

the house, and in the winter it lets in low-angle sunlight to warm the rooms.

Because the architects and owners shared a commitment to using sustainable and salvaged materials, the home is filled with a variety of textures and colors that have the added benefit of being environmentally sound. Eco-friendly materials include plyboo (bamboo hardwood) flooring; redwood decking recycled from the original deck; recycled glass-content kitchen and bath tiles; sustainably harvested Spanish cedar sliding doors; salvaged entry, master suite, and family room doors; recycled glass bathroom

A bay window provides a way to expand a room without altering the foundation or roofline of the building. Here, affordable plywood board-and-batten painted a cheerful shade of blue makes the window an integral part of the exterior design.

The family room had too much dark wood and not enough natural light.

The dining room before the remodel.

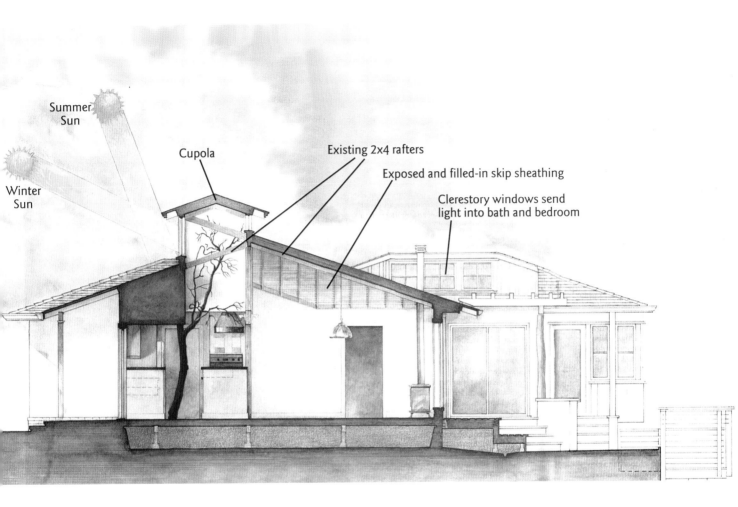

Summer Sun

Winter Sun

Cupola

Existing 2x4 rafters

Exposed and filled-in skip sheathing

Clerestory windows send light into bath and bedroom

The architects tested a scale model of the house on a heliodon, an instrument that simulates the sun's path on any day of the year, to evaluate and adjust the design for maximum daylighting while limiting heat gain during the warmer summer months.

counters; and wall boards saved from another client's demolished garage. The budget was further kept in check with affordable plywood board-and-batten at the added portions, Fireslate counters, and birch cabinets from IKEA.

"The owners were instrumental in how this project turned out," Tilt concludes, "and the product of their hard work is a home that is functional, ecologically sound, and aesthetically rich."

Working with as much of the original structure as possible saved money and retained some of the home's more appealing features. To bring height and light to the interiors, the architects removed the ceiling boards to reveal the solidly built attic structure, filled in the skip sheathing with 1 x 4 boards, and placed a cupola with clerestory windows and louvered vents onto the south side of the roof ridge. Custom Spanish cedar doors on sliding barn-door hardware open the living room to the deck. The Dutch front door was purchased from a salvage yard.

The low ceiling and awkwardly located fireplace made the living room seem smaller than it was.

The condition of the kitchen suggested bold changes.

The kitchen and entry ceilings were kept low to help define functions within the revised floor plan, and a madrone tree harvested by the owners and architects announces the entry and draws the eye up toward the cupola. Fireslate counters and IKEA birch cabinets met budget requirements, and recycled glass-content floor and backsplash tiles were an eco-friendly solution.

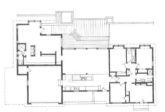

Item of Interest:
The recycled glass-content kitchen and bath tiles are from:
Terra Green Ceramics, Inc.
www.terragreenceramics.com
(765) 935-4760

Sliding doors work well in small floor plans, as illustrated by this salvaged 6-foot x 7-foot glazed door to the family room, formerly the master bedroom. The door slips out from behind a bookcase for acoustic privacy without sacrificing light to the hall.

The hallway to the Girls' Wing extends from the kitchen and entry area and is filled with light thanks to an enlarged opening to the family room, glazed doors, and bright paint.

A salvaged door on off-the-shelf sliding barn-door hardware separates the master suite from the great room.

A cozy window seat faces the canyon behind the house, and high-quality aluminum windows with divided lights set into painted wood frames lend an intimate feel to the room.

Only five feet wide, the master bathroom defies its tiny footprint with high clerestory windows that flood the room with light. Plyboo floors and a terrazzo-like recycled glass countertop on plumbing pipe supports are attractive and environmentally sound choices.

Item of Interest:
The recycled glass bathroom counters are by:
Counter Production
www.counterproduction.com
(510) 843-6916

Blueprint #9

A practical and sturdy but lackluster house steps into the limelight with a dynamic and affordable redo.

Rambler Redux

Seattle, Washington

Cost of Remodel: $100,000 in 1998

Architects: Julie Campbell and Buzz Tenenbom, CTA Design Builders

"Before" Photographs: Courtesy of architects

"After" Photographs: Beverly Multerer

Architects' Transformation Techniques:

—Strategically remove walls on the main level, replacing the enclosed rooms with open, flowing spaces.

—Introduce bold color with a series of planes that draw the eye through the rooms, and keep the decor simple with a pared-down selection of materials including fir, brushed steel, oak, and maple.

—Update the exterior with a shake roof, a larger expanse of windows, and a metal railing.

IF YOU HAVE SPENT TIME in the Northwest, you are probably familiar with ramblers. Placed onto the housing market in the late 1960s and early 1970s, these modest but solidly constructed homes are now ingrained into the landscape of places such as Seattle, and many have been remodeled to take advantage of their admirable qualities and bring them current with today's architectural trends.

Deborah Elvins loves ramblers and recognizes their potential. Soon after purchasing her 1958 home, she hired Julie Campbell and Buzz Tenenbom to design and oversee a remodel that would match her lifestyle and meet her budget. Working with the existing footprint, the architects focused their efforts on a main-level renovation that transformed the choppy 2,200-square-foot floor plan into one that moves effortlessly between spaces.

Previously hidden behind a wall, the stair is now a focal point of the main living area and has been modernized with a cable and teak railing. The original oak floors were restored, and the steel-frame windows were replaced with a fir-veneer variety, a good choice for locales that get lots of rain.

Because the house was structurally sound, the architects didn't have to shore up sagging ceilings or fix other serious problems, which helped keep the budget to a reasonable $100,000. To further save money, Campbell and Tenenbom suggested only subtle exterior revisions meant to "hint at the modernization inside the home," Campbell says.

Before.

The home's footprint was not altered, and the updated exterior is meant to hint at the more dramatic renovation inside. The most noticeable changes are a new shake roof, more (and larger) windows, and a transparent guardrail made of steel posts linked with cable and topped with a teak handrail.

Seattle Remodel

**Residence Remodel at
Seattle, Washington**

Cost of Remodel in 1998: $100,000

Architects: Julie Campbell and Buzz
Tenenbom, CTA Design Builders

Scale: 1″ equals 6′

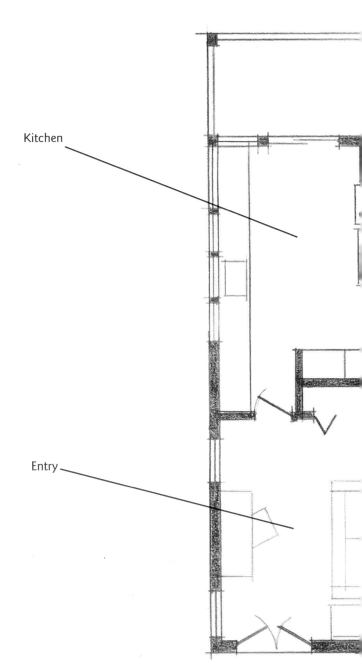

Kitchen

Entry

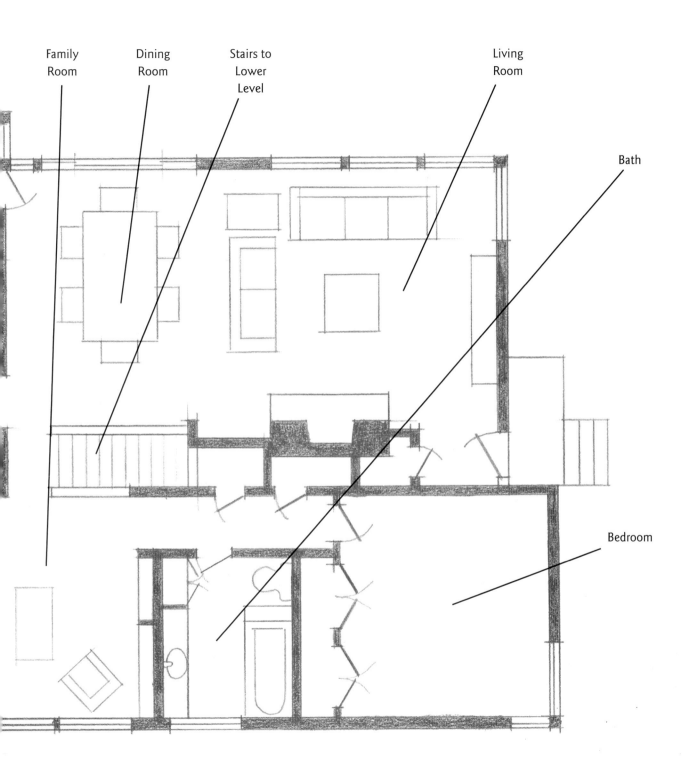

Family
Room

Dining
Room

Stairs to
Lower
Level

Living
Room

Bath

Bedroom

The original living room.

Originally clad in pink tile, the fire-place now has a sleek brushed-steel surround, a dark steel hearth, and a fir mantel. Inner walls in vibrant shades of purple and red establish a series of planes that draw the eye through the expanded spaces and toward the outer wall windows. A wall to the right of the bookshelf alcove was removed to expose the stairway.

Overleaf:

The narrow, galley-type kitchen has been freed of its avocado color scheme, plywood-front cabinets and dire carpet and now features elegant maple cabinets, an oak floor, and large fir-veneer windows and sliders. By extending the counter beyond the cabinetry and supporting it with a simple tapered leg, the architects were able to add, at nominal expense, a built-in dining nook that overlooks the garden.

Durable plastic laminate kitchen counters in lieu of granite saved thousands. The counters, which are black with a brushed patina, resemble the brushed steel found elsewhere in the home and complement the brushed-aluminum sinks. Other distinctive elements include a backsplash of blackened steel tiles patterned with threads of copper, and square drawer and cabinet pulls cut from the backsplash tiles.

The architects began with a reorientation of the layout to give it a more straightforward navigation. "Many ramblers, this one included, have pinched floor plans, but because of the way they are built, with trusses that allow for larger-than-average ceiling spans, it is possible to significantly open them up," Campbell explains. With this in mind, the architects took out two small bedrooms to form a connected family room and living/dining area. Removing a wall exposed the stair, which is now a central part of the plan. Because Elvins often has houseguests, she wanted to be able to accommodate them without compromising her privacy. The new configuration does exactly this: the living/dining area, family room, kitchen, and master suite are on the top floor, while the guest quarters, which received minor finish updates, are downstairs.

The floor-plan puzzle solved, the next step was to tackle the interiors. Typical of the times, the decorating scheme featured pink tile, avocado appliances, a bayberry bathtub and sink, and carpet in the kitchen. To brighten up the rooms and give them a contemporary appearance, the architects assembled a principal palette of fir, steel, and maple—a combination that had the added benefit of tempering costs. To illustrate, although the steel was comparatively expensive, the fir and maple, as well as the Sheetrock walls and plastic laminate counters, helped balance the budget, as did saving and refinishing the original oak floors. White paint on the outer walls and vivid red and purple on the inner walls work together to create a series of planes that draw the eye through the expanded interiors, Campbell explains.

The architects also changed out the steel-frame windows with a fir-veneer variety (a wise option in a damp climate) and installed full-height windows and sliding doors for a more pronounced visual connection to the garden. The kitchen is in the same location but maple cabinets have replaced the plywood-front cabinets and oak has replaced the carpet. Elvins initially wanted granite kitchen counters but discovered they were too pricey. The architects proposed an attractive and affordable alternative: $500 plastic laminate manufactured to resemble brushed steel. Visible on the home's exterior are a new shake roof, a steel-and-cable guardrail in place of a solid rail, and a reworked window placement.

"Deborah had a fairly modest budget and certainly didn't want a trophy house," Campbell concludes. "All it took was a few simple moves and a careful selection of materials to give her a home that is both casual and elegant and easily welcomes family and friends."

The bathroom's bayberry-and-pink color scheme, popular in 1958, has been replaced with white tile and fir cabinets. The small bathroom feels larger thanks to windows that open to a deck.

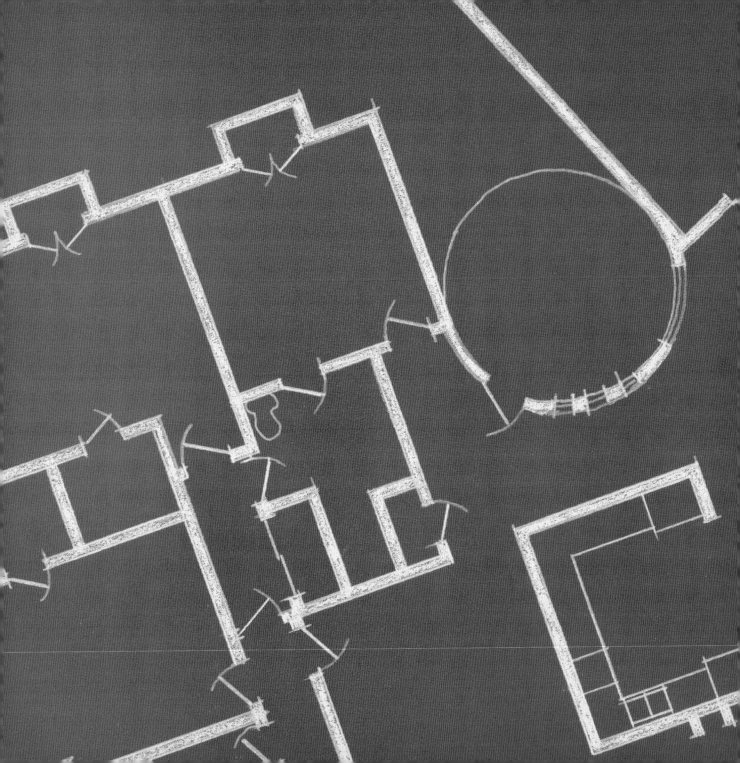

Blueprint # 10

*A 1960s ranch grows up
with a remodel that fills its
spaces with sophisticated
features and forms.*

From Cutesy to Classy

Los Altos, California

Cost of Remodel: $225,000 in 2000

Architect: Mark English, Mark English Architects

"Before" Photographs: Courtesy of architect

"After" Photographs: Claudio Santini ("after" master bathroom photo by Alan Geller)

Architect's Transformation Techniques:

—Maintain the one-level elevation and preserve the existing roofline, removing the low ceilings inside to tap into the unused attic space.

—Take out as few walls as possible to minimize construction costs and rework the floor plan for easy circulation free from "roadblocks" and "dead-ends."

—Keep interiors simple, for a clean backdrop for artwork and furniture.

ONCE AGAIN, we have a less-than-ideal tract house in a desirable location—in this case, the San Francisco suburb of Los Altos. Built in 1964, this ranch-style home was undeniably cute, with its "cottage-y" detailing, pale green stucco, and wood shake roof. Inside, however, its claustrophobic layout and lifeless décor desperately needed an overhaul. "When I saw the house for the first time, I noticed a few good things, namely a Japanese maple tree near the entrance and a well-landscaped backyard," says architect Mark English. "But inside it was awful."

Originally 1,630 square feet, the home's floor plan was what you might expect: closed-off rooms and tight circulation patterns. Now 3,000 square feet, the house has been reborn—gone are the bland color scheme and poorly executed spatial relationships, replaced with modest but graceful

The master bedroom sits apart from the main spaces and has French doors that open to a private patio. The architect combined square and gable roof forms for variety and contrast but maintained the original roof height.

The front of the 1964 house before the remodel.

The back of the house wraps around a patio accessed through the dining room's French doors and the glass doors in the family room. The exterior walls have been given a fresh coat of light-gray, integral-color stucco infused with a purple tint for a timeless appearance inspired by the buildings the architect studied during his academic travels in Italy. Operable and fixed aluminum windows painted in a long-lasting powder-coat require less maintenance than wood.

Before, a breezeway connected the garage to the house, and the narrow kitchen door was the sole opening to the backyard.

Floorplan Before Remodel

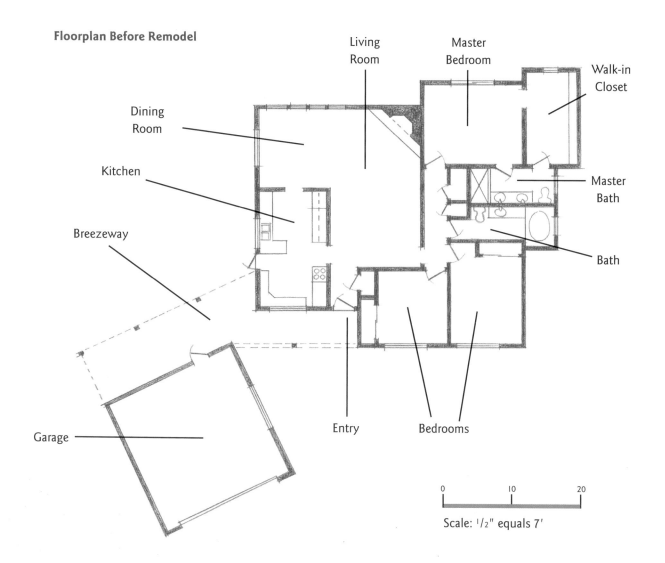

Living
Room

Master
Bedroom

Walk-in
Closet

Dining
Room

Kitchen

Master
Bath

Breezeway

Bath

Garage

Entry

Bedrooms

0   10   20

Scale: $^1/_2$" equals 7'

Floorplan After Remodel

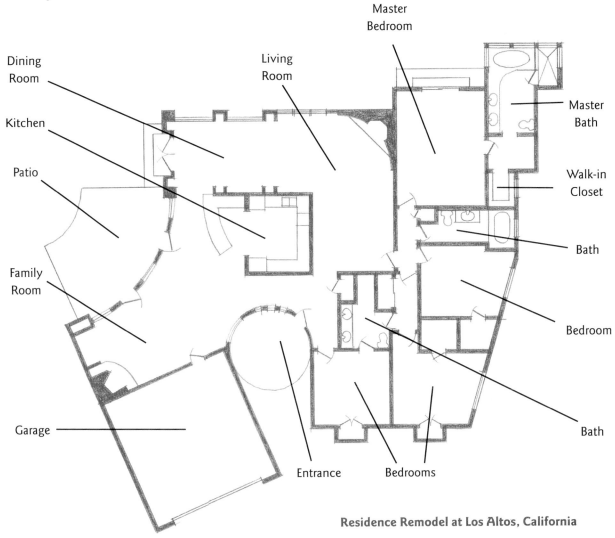

Master Bedroom

Dining Room

Living Room

Kitchen

Master Bath

Patio

Walk-in Closet

Family Room

Bath

Bedroom

Garage

Bath

Entrance

Bedrooms

Residence Remodel at Los Altos, California

Cost of Remodel in 2000: $225,000

Architect: Mark English, Mark English Architects

materials and rooms that speak a common language. "The owners wanted a low-maintenance house that could easily accommodate indoor and outdoor entertaining," English explains. "And they needed spaces that would encourage unrestricted movement, without any dead-ends or roadblocks along the way. The main problem with the house before the remodel was that once you were in these rooms, there was nowhere to go—you were stuck."

For budget reasons, English worked as much as possible with the existing structural composition and kept the roofline; the latter also meant he didn't have to seek permission from the building department to raise the height of the roof. He filled in the garage breezeway with a family room addition that opens to the backyard patio via slim glass doors, and

Low ceilings made the living room look dark and uninviting, and a painted masonry fireplace did little to liven up the room.

Item of Interest:
The fine art and sculpture depicted in the photographs were provided by:
ArtHaus
www.arthaus-sf.com

Because the fireplace could not be moved due to building code restrictions, the architect hid its unattractive masonry behind a delicately curving Sheetrock wall that rises with the ceiling. This cost-effective technique makes it seem as if the fireplace is emerging from the wall.

A curved piece of granite rests on an Anigre-veneer counter that acts as both an informal dining table and a work surface that allows the cook to interact with others while in the kitchen. The floors here and throughout the home are red oak with a clear finish, and the Sheetrock walls were trimmed with bullnosed corner beams for an aesthetic rounding at the edges. Italian glass light fixtures add a stylish touch.

The original kitchen was cramped and closed off from the rest of the house.

relocated the front entry. The green stucco gave way to a light gray integral-color version infused with a subtle purple tint.

Inside, English realized he could lift the volumes by capturing the unused attic space; indeed, removing the ceiling boards and exposing the attic allowed him to raise the ceiling height by as much as 14 feet in some areas, a significant increase over the standard 8 feet found in this and many other tract houses. From there, he turned his attention to what he describes as a series of "events": a dining room with a temple-like quality, a

The kitchen walls are a rich red to reflect what the architect describes as "the heart of the house," and the cabinets are affordable eastern maple. Black plastic laminate was used for the cornice on top of the cabinets and for the floor band. Halogen lights placed under the top cabinets cast a warm glow on the granite counters.

Tall windows open to the patio and keep the interiors filled with sunlight, and the upper lights are operable awnings for enhanced ventilation. The columns between the windows are curved at the top to avoid an abrupt stop at the ceiling, and light from the alabaster sconces shines up on the columns, emphasizing their shape. The architect was able to raise the ceilings without increasing the roof height by tapping into the unused attic volume above the old ceiling boards. Glulam ridge beams now support the roof.

Item of Interest:
The alabaster sconces on the family room wall are by:
Artemide
www.artemide.com

The architect gave the dining room a temple-like quality by setting it apart from the living and family room in a space with a cathedral ceiling, tall windows, and French doors. The small square window above the French doors offers diners a framed glimpse of sky.

Item of Interest:

The living room furniture and
dining table and chairs are by:
Donghia
212.925.2777
www.donghia.com

kitchen painted a sultry shade of red, and curved columns to divide the family room windows. One of the home's most distinctive elements is in the living room. Because the building code dictated that the fireplace stay put, English conceived an affordable and attractive way to address its clunky painted masonry surround: he disguised it with a curving Sheetrock wall that rises with the ceiling from 8 to 12 feet.

Overall, English focused on making the updated forms of the house exciting while keeping the backdrop simple, so that

A square window in the master bedroom has been positioned similarly to the one in the dining room. French doors, luminous paint, and a cathedral ceiling dramatically changed the personality of the room.

artwork, designer furniture, and well-tended plants could enjoy the limelight. The architect's materials palette included commercial aluminum windows, red oak floors coated with a clear finish, an Anigre-veneer bar counter topped with Baltic brown granite, maple kitchen cabinets, and slate tile.

"I enjoy the challenge of tract homes," English says. "It's really about trying to make something beautiful out of a structure that is anything but extraordinary. I see more and more of this type of work—land is so expensive here that refurbishing a tract house makes a lot of sense."

Overleaf:

The revamped master bathroom is roomy enough for a large tub and steam shower. The flooring and tub deck are Chinese green slate cut into 8 x 16 rectangles from 16 x 16 tiles, and the cabinets are quilted maple veneer with a countertop of Baltic brown granite finished with a simple polished edge. The walls are glazed with a gray-green oil wash.

Finding an Architect

You are ready to transform your tract house and have decided to hire an architect. Here are a few tips for selecting the right professional to help you remodel your home:

1. Interview several architects before you make a decision, and remember that some charge fees for interviews.

2. Ask the architects you're interviewing for the names of clients who would be willing to share their experiences.

3. If possible, visit a home your architect has remodeled so you can get a sense of his approach to the particular challenges of tract houses.

4. Make sure you know the rules and guidelines that pertain to remodeling in your neighborhood. Call the local building department for suggestions and direction.

5. Research the architect's license and other professional credentials and/or awards.

6. To facilitate better communication with your architect, take the time to develop an understanding about architecture and building techniques. You don't have to be an expert, but the more you know, the more comfortable you will be with the process. (And it will be more fun, too.)

7. Chances are your remodel will have to adhere to a budget, so take the time to learn as much as possible about cost-effective building materials and techniques. The Internet is an excellent source of this kind of information.

Resources

National Association of the
Remodeling Industry (NARI)
780 Lee Street, Suite 200
Des Plaines, IL 60016
800-611-NARI (6274)
www.nari.org

American Institute
of Architects (AIA)
1735 New York Avenue NW
Washington, DC 20006
(800) AIA-3837
www.aia.org
www.aiaonline.com

Architecture Research
Institute
29 Broadway, Suite 1100
New York, NY 10006
(212) 344-0400
www.architect.org

National Association of
Home Builders
Research Center
400 Prince George's
Boulevard
Upper Marlboro, MD 20774
(800) 638-8556
www.nahbrc.org

American Institute
of Building Design
2505 Main Street, Suite
209B
Stratford, CT 06615
(800) 366-2423
www.aibd.org

Internet-Based Resources

Although these listings represent only
a fraction of what you can find on the
Internet, they will give you a good
starting point.

www.ebuild.com
(extensive guide to building products)

www.remodelingmagazine.com

www.hometime.com

www.home-remodeling-directory.com

www.homeremodelingonline.com

Architects

David Arkin
Anni Tilt
Arkin Tilt Architects
1101 8th Street, Suite 180
Berkeley, CA 94710
(510) 528-9830
www.arkintilt.com

Charles Bernstein
M. Charles Bernstein Architects
1734-A Topanga Skyline Drive
Topanga, CA 90290
(310) 260-4731
www.mcharlesbernstein.com

Randy Brown
Randy Brown Architects
1925 North 120th Street
Omaha, NE 68154
(402) 551-7097
www.randybrownarchitects.com

Julie Campbell
Buzz Tenenbom
CTA Design Builders
2556 11th Avenue West
Seattle, WA 98119
(206) 286-1692
www.ctabuilds.com

Mark English
Mark English Architects
250 Columbus Street, Suite 200
San Francisco, CA 94133
(415) 391-0186
www.markenglisharchitects.com

Grant Kirkpatrick
Kirkpatrick Associates Architects
4201 Redwood Avenue
Los Angeles, CA 90066
(310) 821-1400
www.kaadesigngroup.com

Elissa Morgante
Fred Wilson
Morgante Wilson Architects
3813 North Ravenswood
Chicago, IL 60613
(773) 528-1001
www.morgantewilson.com

Hugh Jefferson Randolph
Hugh Jefferson Randolph Architect
1215 West 5th Street
Austin, TX 78703
(512) 474-7030

John Sofio
Built, Inc.
7257 Beverly Boulevard
Los Angeles, CA 90036
(323) 857-0409
www.builtinc.com

Architect/Photographer Listings

Photographers

David Adamson
Harriet Robinson
Lone Pine Pictures
6944 Langdon Avenue
Van Nuys, CA 91406
(818) 785-9313
www.lonepinepictures.net

Farshid Assassi
Assassi Productions
Architectural Photography
P.O. Box 3651
Santa Barbara, CA 93130
(805) 895-7703
www.assassi.com

Weldon Brewster
Weldon Brewster Photography
4028 Chaney Trail
Altadena, CA 91001
(626) 296-0190
www.weldonbrewster.com

Edward Caldwell
Location Photography
1783 29th Avenue
San Francisco, CA 94122
(415) 664-9873
www.edwardcaldwell.com

Robert Millman
P.O. Box 3566
Aspen, CO 81612
(970) 923-6511

Beverly Multerer
4509 Interlake Avenue North, #302
Seattle, WA 98103
(206) 595-8535

Hilary Rose
1093 Princeton Avenue
Highland Park, IL 60035
(847) 831-2484

Claudio Santini
Architectural Photography
12915 Greene Avenue
Los Angeles, CA 90066
(310) 578-7919
www.claudiosantini.com